INTO THE DEEP

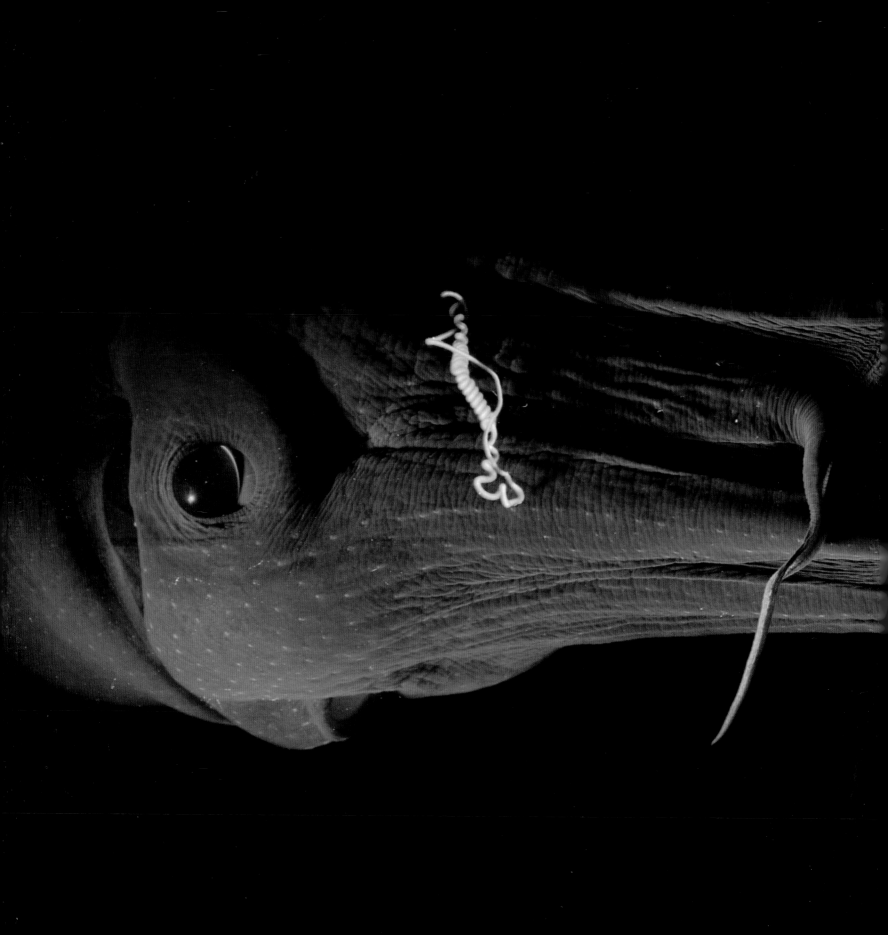

INTO THE DEEP

Karsten Schneider & Peter Batson

Quercus

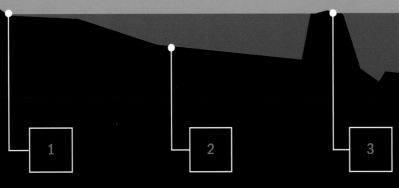

16 AT THE FRINGES

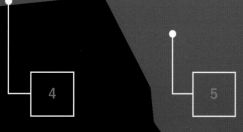

Foreword

by Don Walsh

THE WORLD OCEAN: the single largest geographic feature on our poorly named planet, 'Earth'.

For most, it is difficult to comprehend the ocean's breadths and depths, let alone the splendid diversity of its life. The surface area of the Pacific Ocean alone is greater than all the Earth's continental landmasses put together. The world ocean's average depth is about four kilometres, with the deepest places being in the Pacific. It is here that the ocean plunges to its maximum depth of 10,911 metres in the Challenger Deep near the island of Guam – where my own brush with history took place in 1960, aboard the bathyscaphe *Trieste*.

One statistic that is particularly difficult to grasp is the volume of living space hidden away in the depths: 338 million cubic miles. To give some scale to this huge number, the entire population of our planet, about six billion people, could fit into less than one cubic mile.

Into the Deep is aimed squarely at general readers of all ages. The journey begins in shallow coastal areas, where most people have first experienced the sea, then moves progressively further from the shoreline and into the abyss where only a handful of explorers have gone.

A place of ongoing exploration and discovery, the ocean remains an exciting challenge for the next generation of scientists. There is much left to be done and this will be the situation for many decades to come.

Pick up *Into the Deep*; I hope you will find it a good addition to your bookshelf. Come join the journey to the 'inner space' of our planet.

RIGHT *Observed from space, hovering high above the Pacific Ocean, our planet reveals its true – watery – nature. Almost no land is in sight and it is a somewhat surprising fact that oceans cover more than 70 percent of the Earth's surface.*

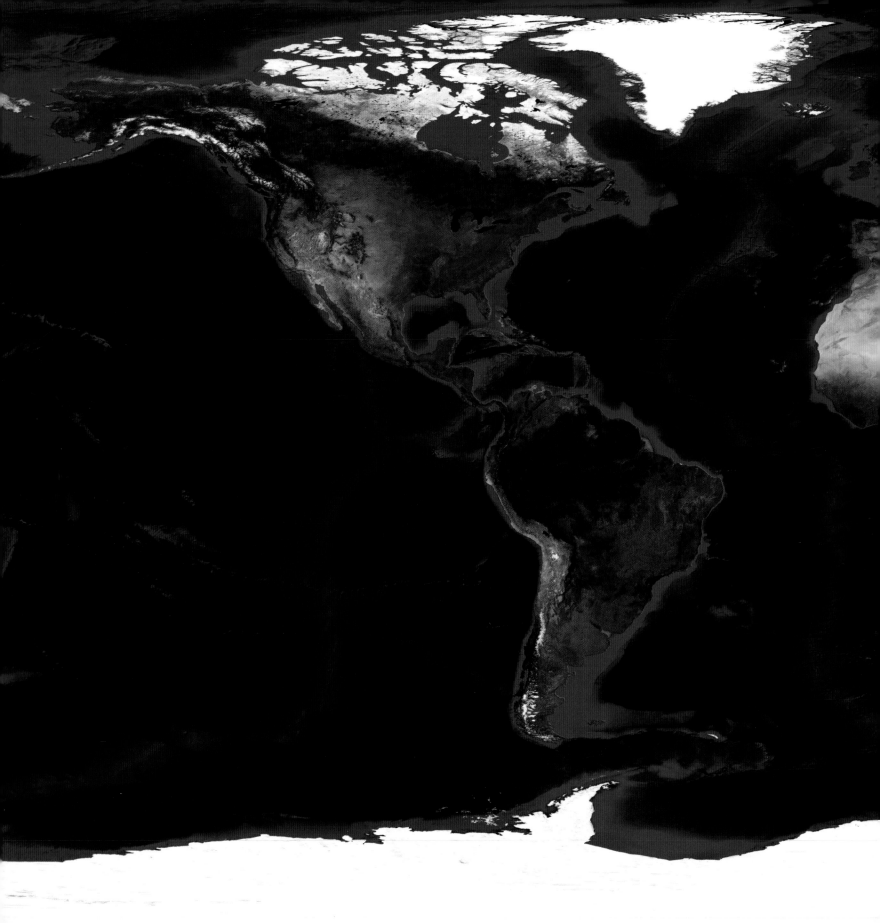

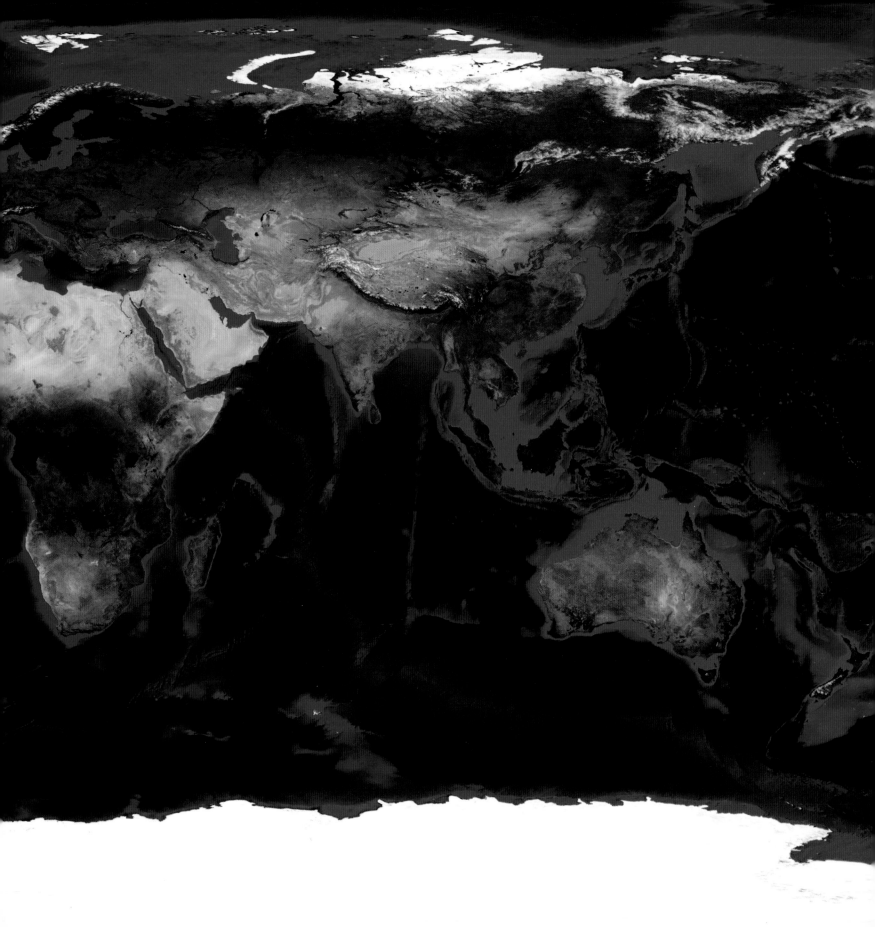

Introduction

EARTH – IT REALLY IS THE WRONG NAME for our blue planet. We are so used to seeing satellite images with continental land masses filling the view, but picture the Earth from space, high above the Pacific, and almost all you can see is water. A long-haul flight across the Pacific from Sydney, Australia, to Los Angeles takes 12 hours at 1,000 kilometres an hour – and it's ocean all the way. More than 70 percent of the planet's surface is covered by ocean.

The ocean is the cradle of life. Here is where it all began. When the young Earth had cooled down from the red-hot furnace of its birth, water began to condense in clouds. It began to rain and didn't stop for millennia. By the end of that deluge water had filled the deep depressions on the Earth's surface, forming the first ocean.

As if waiting in the wings, with the ocean came life. The earliest signs of life that are still visible today are microbial cities that bacteria built in warm shallow seas 3,800 million years ago, just 100 million years after the Earth's crust was formed. Once the microbes had taken over the sea they branched out, becoming more and more sophisticated. Some invented ways to feed off sunlight and in the process created the oxygen atmosphere of our planet. Single cells learned to work together to form colonies, then specialized and became parts of other cells. Eventually those cells specialized even further and became part of multi-cellular bodies. All the groups of animals and plants we know today had their origins in the ocean. That includes us. In fact we still carry a little bit of the ancient ocean in our bodies today – the salt in our tears points back to a time in our history when our ancestors were still living beneath the waves and had to cope with a salty environment.

The reason for the rapid proliferation of life in the ocean is largely due to some very special attributes of water, making it the essence of life. Its chemical and physical properties are truly extraordinary. Its unique molecular structure makes it the almost universal solvent, providing cells with a medium within which the complex chemistry of life can take place. Most organisms contain more than 60 percent water and some – like the marine jellies – are 95 percent water.

Out of reach of the warming sun, ice would accumulate on the seabed, causing oceans and lakes in the polar regions to freeze solid from the bottom up – killing almost all aquatic life in the process. A frozen polar ocean would disable the vital exchange of water masses with tropical regions. The tropics would lose their 'water-cooler' and as a result become hotter – unbearably hot for life in fact. Luckily for us, and for all life on Earth, water does not behave like other substances.

Water has a great capacity to store heat. Containing over 96 percent of all water on the planet, the ocean is a vital global buffer against temperature extremes. It takes a lot of energy to boil the water in a kettle, and once the kettle has boiled, it takes along time for the water to return to its original temperature. Similarly, the ocean absorbs solar energy when the sun shines and very slowly releases it when the sun is hidden, minimizing temperature differences between day and night, between summer and winter. That is why coastlines experience a much milder climate than the continental interior, with cooler summers and warmer winters. Without water's ability to cushion temperatures in this way, the nights would be freezing cold and the days unbearably hot in tropical and temperate regions alike.

Interactions between water and sunlight also fuel the largest machine on Earth – the weather engine. Water and heat are constantly being exchanged between atmosphere and ocean. Heated by intense solar radiation surface waters, especially in the tropics, evaporate into the atmosphere. This water vapour forms clouds that shade and cool the ocean like sweat cools the body of a jogger. Throw salt into the mix and you have the weather machine that drives our climate. The evaporating seawater around the equator leaves its salt content behind, making the remaining seawater denser and so it begins to sink into the deep. Oceanographers call these sinks 'downwellings'. Neighbouring surface water moves horizontally into the region where the sinking occurs, and elsewhere water has to rise to replace the water that moves horizontally, forming an upwelling and thus completing the cycle: an ocean current is

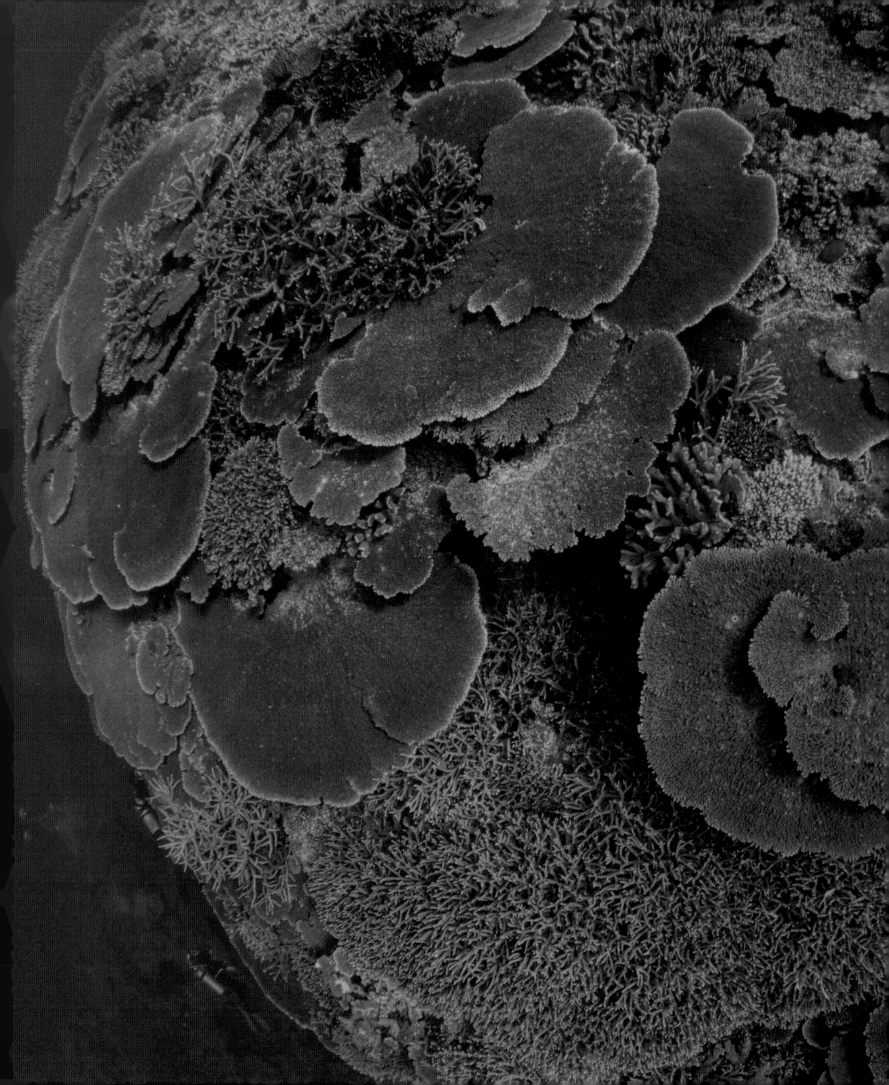

open water deserts congregate in their own hot spots, which can be an upwelling, a seamount, an atoll, or even around a little life raft of seaweed or driftwood. The rich and colourful communities here have to make do with very little and are prime practitioners of very efficient recycling. Every food scrap, every organism that dies is instantly taken up and reintroduced into the food-web. Contrast this with the abundance of life in the open ocean of the polar region where plankton provides the greatest accumulation of biomass in the sea, enabling even the largest whales to feed.

Finally, we dive into the deep sea – the dominant habitat on the planet. It is dark, the temperature is cold but constant, and the pressure is enormous. Conditions in the deep sea provide a dramatic contrast to the dynamic changing world of shallow coastal habitats. Our journey through the habitats of the ocean goes from shallow into the deep, but also from diverse to unified. Many of the creatures living down here can be found anywhere in the world ocean, provided it is deep enough. Species that have been discovered in the dark reaches of the ocean are just as diverse and beautiful in their own bizarre ways as the life close to the surface.

For a long time very little was known about the ocean in general, and the deep ocean in particular. The expedition of HMS *Challenger* from 1872 to 1876 marked the beginning of modern oceanography and the first serious attempt to find out about the life in the deep sea. Exciting new research technologies were developed after the Second World War, when sonar, scuba diving, submarines, and satellite technology finally opened new windows to observe and understand the inner workings of the ocean.

Although our knowledge about the ocean has vastly improved during the course of the last century, the deep sea is still largely unexplored. The deepest ocean depth that has ever been sounded is in the Challenger Deep basin of the Mariana Trench at a depth of 10,911 metres (35,798 feet) below sea level. It has been visited just once, in January 1960, by Jacques Piccard and Don Walsh on board the bathyscaphe *Trieste*. More humans have visited the moon than have been to the deepest part of the ocean.

The other great geographical extreme on Earth – the highest mountain, Mount Everest – has become a magnet for climbers from around the world since it was first scaled in 1953 by Sir Edmund Hillary and Tenzing Norgay. Scores of mountaineers make their way to the summit each year, but nobody has ever been back down to the Challenger Deep. Consider the scale of these two opposing frontiers – sink Mount Everest in the Challenger Deep and there would still be two kilometres of water between its summit and the surface of the ocean.

The contrast in visitor numbers to these two geographical extremes is due to one main factor – pressure. While climbers lining up for Mount Everest can train themselves to deal with the thin air at high altitude – even to the point of leaving their oxygen supply at home – visiting the deepest parts of the ocean requires the construction and deployment of special vehicles capable of withstanding the crushing pressures of the deep ocean. At the bottom of the Mariana Trench the pressure is over a thousand times greater than at the ocean surface. Currently, there is not one single submersible, bathyscaphe or remotely operated vehicle in the world that is capable of diving deeper than 7,000 metres. Today, when the surface of Mars has been photographed by satellite down to a resolution of fractions of a metre, only five percent of Earth's ocean floor has been mapped in any detail.

New oceanic creatures are still discovered on a regular basis. In 2007 the largest colossal squid ever recorded was caught by a commercial fishing boat off the Antarctic coast south of New Zealand. At 450 kilograms it was more than double the weight of any other large squid caught before, and at ten metres it was longer than a London double-decker bus. It had a tongue studded with razor-sharp teeth and each tentacle ended in a club covered with mean talon-like swivelling hooks. Even today sea-monsters of that size, and possibly even bigger, are still lurking in the deep, waiting to be discovered. The deep ocean remains a potent symbol of the final frontier, beckoning further exploration.

The ocean has fascinated humankind through the ages. When the Earth was considered to be flat the ocean provided the border to the underworld – the edge over which you would plunge if you dared to venture too far. It was considered to be filled with gods and with sea-monsters, awe-inspiring and frightening. But it also was the great provider, offering limitless amounts of food, even the prospect of new lands, to those who risked its perilous waves. In some ways, perhaps, not much has changed in our modern minds. Sea-monsters are still out there – only today we try to take photos of them. We still seem to have the impression that the food supply from the sea is limitless, although collapsing fish stocks around the world prove otherwise. We have passed the goalpost of sustainability a long time ago and can only hope that fish stocks will be able to recover once international agreements for their protection are reached. But life still thrives, making the most of the different physical constraints: beautiful, ingenious, sometimes bizarre but always amazing.

In this book we will showcase examples of marine life's spectacular capability to adapt and to survive against the odds. With carefully selected images by some of the world's best natural history photographers, this book is a celebration of life in the ocean. Below each animal depicted there is a panel listing its common name, species name, size and distribution. For larger animals, such as whales or sharks, the size given is that attained by a fully-grown individual. For smaller fishes and invertebrate animals – many of which change form and colour dramatically as they grow – we have indicated the approximate size of the animal in the photograph. Where known, the distribution of each species is provided as a map showing their approximate range. In some cases the species was uncertain and the distribution of the species' genus or family is given instead.

RIGHT *With markings reminiscent of Aboriginal art, the impressive bulk of a whale shark emerges from clear oceanic waters.*

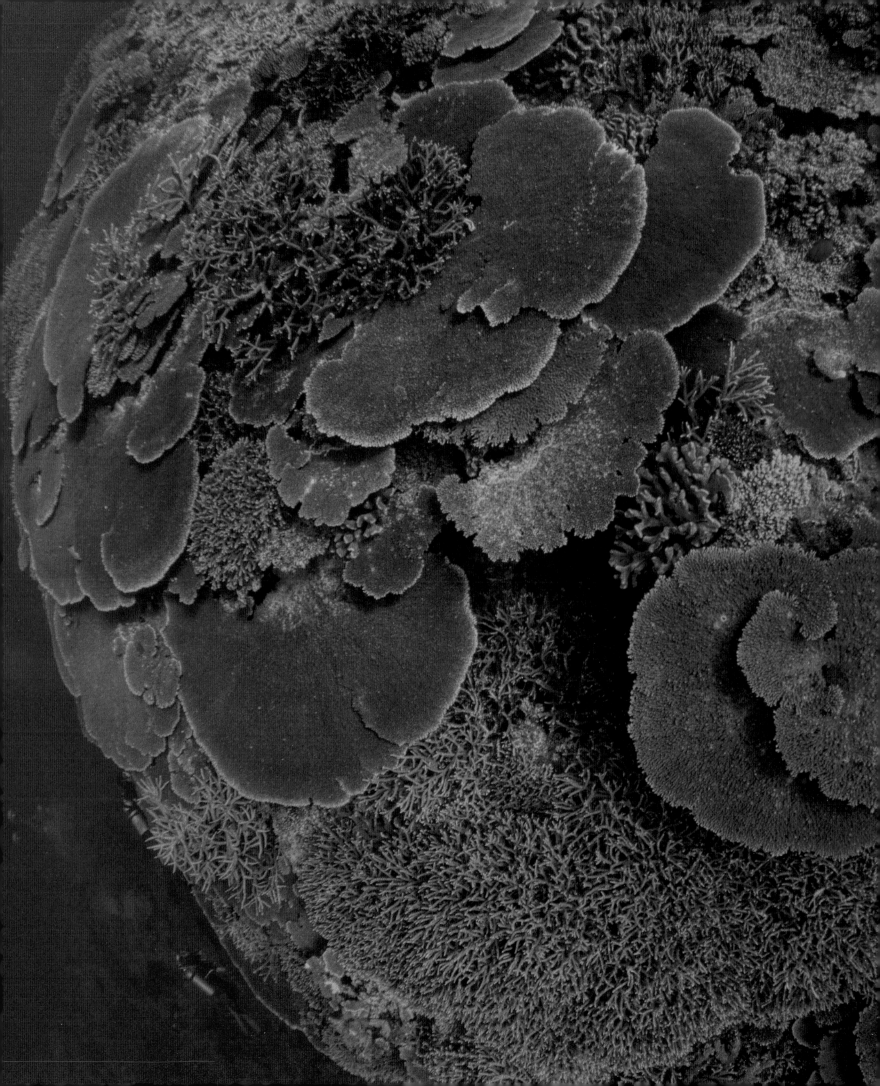

formed, driven by solar power. Imagine these movements of water on a global scale. Like giant conveyor belts, currents move energy and nutrients around the world. The movement of water around the planet and between the deep and the surface balances temperatures worldwide, while upwellings bring a payload of sediments and nutrients from the deep, feeding the plankton that support a multitude of species at the ocean surface.

The oceans are by far the largest habitat on the planet with about 300 times more living space available than on land, but the greatest density of life is found near the surface and close to land. This crowding leads to fierce competition for resources and one might wonder why life is not more evenly distributed through the ocean. The reason lies in yet another special property of water – it absorbs sunlight and therefore limits the depth to which light can penetrate the water column. Water breaks the incoming sunlight into its different components, absorbing the long waves of red light directly at the surface. Only a little further down, yellow and then green are gone. The short waves of blue light penetrate the deepest, giving the characteristic bluish tint familiar to divers and snorkellers, but at a depth of 200 metres even that residual light has gone and it is pitch black.

However, almost all life depends on sunlight – either directly via photosynthesis or indirectly by consuming plants or bacteria that convert light into energy. Just as plants on land compete with each other for optimum exposure to sunlight, so phytoplankton and seaweeds must ensure they find a place in the sun. The topmost 30 metres of the water column is a crowded place.

Shallow waters close to the coast offer additional attractions to life. Phytoplankton and seaweeds have an urgent need for minerals to build their cells and tissues. Just like lettuces in a garden plot they need nitrogen, phosphorus and other essential nutrients. These elements are most abundant in coastal waters where freshwater run-off from the land after rain and the sediment load of rivers carry salts and minerals into the oceans. Coastal waters also provide physical refuges. Rocks, sand and mud provide shelter from predators, or an anchor-point – a quality that is not only appreciated by plants, but also by many animals that attach themselves to a surface so they can sieve the currents for plankton.

Some species have chosen habitats that are less crowded – and there is no shortage of space out there in the open ocean, from the sun-lit surface down to the perpetual darkness and crushing pressures of the abyss. There are no solid boundaries in this huge watery realm, the creatures that live here have no firm surface to attach to, they cannot burrow, there is no place to hide. But at least they don't have to contend with the coastal risks of being pulverized by waves on the shore or of running out of water to breathe. The main challenges are to stay afloat and avoid being eaten.

Certain very small planktonic organisms have developed intricate appendages, which increase their resistance to sinking. Some store fat droplets to further improve their buoyancy, since fat is less dense than water. Even the largest whales use their substantial oily blubber to assist buoyancy. Most fish have taken a different pathway and use the buoyancy of air-filled swim bladders to regulate their depth in the water column. Control of the gas content of their swim bladders allows some fish to undertake daily vertical migrations of many hundreds of metres within the water column, rising towards the surface to feed at dusk and descending into the protective darkness at dawn. This is the biggest regular daily movement of biomass on the planet, a 500-million-ton biological piston.

Open ocean dwellers are very exposed, there is nowhere to hide. To avoid becoming a meal requires evasion of the sharp eyes of predators and, in true military style, camouflage and stealth can provide a solution. Many small creatures such as jellies and some crustaceans are translucent and almost as invisible as Harry Potter wearing his cloak. Other animals use complicated patterns of counter-shading to break up their body forms, or even employ adjustable light organs on their underside to match the bright ocean surface when viewed by predators from below – instead of presenting a dark silhouetted target.

The use of light organs plays an even more important role in deep-sea communities where bioluminescence is used to confuse predators or as a lure to attract prey. The deep-sea floor itself offers attractions in patches that we are only just beginning to understand. Deep-sea hydrothermal vents, cold seeps and even rotting whale carcasses have their own highly specialized communities, thriving in an otherwise quite featureless and nutrient poor environment. These are true oases of life in the desert of the abyss.

These examples show that life is not distributed evenly throughout the oceans but is concentrated in hot spots. Hot spots offer an amazing insight into the diversity and ingenuity of life. There are arms races going on between predators and prey, heavy competition for food and mates amongst members of the same species – but also beautiful and touching arrangements of mutual support between often unlikely neighbours.

This book looks at these different communities, at the hot spots of life. We take you on a journey from the coast into the ocean deeps. We start at the interface between the ocean and the land – the intertidal zone of the coast. Life here is extremely hard, because organisms have to cope with huge fluctuations in temperature and salinity. They may be exposed to air for many hours during low tide. It takes specialists of the hardy kind to make a living in this environment. Moving a little further out into shallow coastal waters we discover a huge variety of habitats. From rocky cliff faces to sandy bottoms, from coral reefs in the tropics to the underside of ice floes in the Arctic – each one of these habitats poses its own challenges to the communities that carve out a living here.

From the fringes we move out into the open ocean. We stay close to the surface and explore the sun-drenched top layer of the oceans. Here we have huge open spaces with very little life in the tropics. Organisms in these blue open water deserts congregate in their own hot spots, which can be an upwelling, a seamount, an atoll, or even around a little life raft of seaweed or driftwood. The rich and colourful communities here have to make do with very little and are prime practitioners of very efficient recycling. Every food scrap, every organism that dies is instantly taken up and reintroduced into the food-web. Contrast this with the abundance of life in the open ocean of the polar region where plankton provides the greatest accumulation of biomass in the sea, enabling even the largest whales to feed.

Finally, we dive into the deep sea – the dominant habitat on the planet. It is dark, the temperature is cold but constant, and the pressure is enormous. Conditions in the deep sea provide a dramatic contrast to the dynamic changing world of shallow coastal habitats. Our journey through the habitats of the ocean goes from shallow into the deep, but also from diverse to unified. Many of the creatures living down here can be found anywhere in the world ocean, provided it is deep enough. Species that have been discovered in the dark reaches of the ocean are just as diverse and beautiful in their own bizarre ways as the life close to the surface.

For a long time very little was known about the ocean in general, and the deep ocean in particular. The expedition of HMS *Challenger* from 1872 to 1876 marked the beginning of modern oceanography and the first serious attempt to find out about the life in the deep sea. Exciting new research technologies were developed after the Second World War, when sonar, scuba diving, submarines and satellite technology finally opened new windows to observe and understand the inner workings of the ocean.

Although our knowledge about the ocean has vastly improved during the course of the last century, the deep sea is still largely unexplored. The deepest ocean depth that has ever been sounded is in the Challenger Deep basin of the Mariana Trench at a depth of 10,911 metres (35,798 feet) below sea level. It has been visited just once, in January 1960, by Jacques Piccard and Don Walsh on board the bathyscaphe *Trieste*. More humans have visited the moon than have been to the deepest part of the ocean.

The other great geographical extreme on Earth – the highest mountain, Mount Everest – has become a magnet for climbers from around the world since it was first scaled in 1953 by Sir Edmund Hillary and Tenzing Norgay. Scores of mountaineers make their way to the summit each year, but nobody has ever been back down to the Challenger Deep. Consider the scale of these two opposing frontiers – sink Mount Everest in the Challenger Deep and there would still be two kilometres of water between its summit and the surface of the ocean.

The contrast in visitor numbers to these two geographical extremes is due to one main factor – pressure. While climbers lining up for Mount Everest can train themselves to deal with the thin air at high altitude – even to the point of leaving their oxygen supply at home – visiting the deepest parts of the ocean requires the construction and deployment of special vehicles capable of withstanding the crushing pressures of the deep ocean. At the bottom of the Mariana Trench the pressure is over a thousand times greater than at the ocean surface. Currently, there is not one single submersible, bathyscaphe or

remotely operated vehicle in the world that is capable of diving deeper than 7,000 metres. Today, when the surface of Mars has been photographed by satellite down to a resolution of fractions of a metre, only five percent of Earth's ocean floor has been mapped in any detail.

New oceanic creatures are still discovered on a regular basis. In 2007 the largest colossal squid ever recorded was caught by a commercial fishing boat off the Antarctic coast south of New Zealand. At 450 kilograms it was more than double the weight of any other large squid caught before, and at ten metres it was longer than a London double-decker bus. It had a tongue studded with razor-sharp teeth and each tentacle ended in a club covered with mean talon-like swivelling hooks. Even today sea-monsters of that size, and possibly even bigger, are still lurking in the deep, waiting to be discovered. The deep ocean remains a potent symbol of the final frontier, beckoning further exploration.

The ocean has fascinated humankind through the ages. When the Earth was considered to be flat the ocean provided the border to the underworld – the edge over which you would plunge if you dared to venture too far. It was considered to be filled with gods and with sea-monsters, awe-inspiring and frightening. But it also was the great provider, offering limitless amounts of food, even the prospect of new lands, to those who risked its perilous waves. In some ways, perhaps, not much has changed in our modern minds. Sea-monsters are still out there – only today we try to take photos of them. We still seem to have the impression that the food supply from the sea is limitless, although collapsing fish stocks around the world prove otherwise. We have passed the goalpost of sustainability a long time ago and can only hope that fish stocks will be able to recover once international agreements for their protection are reached. But life still thrives, making the most of the different physical constraints: beautiful, ingenious, sometimes bizarre but always amazing.

In this book we will showcase examples of marine life's spectacular capability to adapt and to survive against the odds. With carefully selected images by some of the world's best natural history photographers, this book is a celebration of life in the ocean. Below each animal depicted there is a panel listing its common name, species name, size and distribution. For larger animals, such as whales or sharks, the size given is that attained by a fully-grown individual. For smaller fishes and invertebrate animals – many of which change form and colour dramatically as they grow – we have indicated the approximate size of the animal in the photograph. Where known, the distribution of each species is provided as a map showing their approximate range. In some cases the species was uncertain and the distribution of the species' genus or family is given instead.

RIGHT *With markings reminiscent of Aboriginal art, the impressive bulk of a whale shark emerges from clear oceanic waters.*

AT THE FRINGES

LEFT What seems like an alien landscape is just a familiar coastline captured in a long-exposure photo. The waves, the surf, the spray, all are blurred, indicating the constant motion of the ocean. Even the rocks that seem so steady and permanent are eroded over time.

1 Life at the Edge

N PERPETUAL FLUX, THE COAST is the most dynamic of all the ocean's environments. Waves and weather are relentlessly shaping it, eroding a rocky shore here and depositing pebbles or finely ground sand on a beach over there. Huge loads of sediments are carried into the ocean by rivers and streams, globally an estimated 20 billion tons each year – more than 3,000 times the weight of the great pyramid at Giza. The sediments are deposited in estuaries, in ever-growing deltas or along the coast, only to be picked up again later by the wave action of a stormy ocean.

These movements have been the same ever since the first oceans formed four billion years ago. To a time traveller, Earth's first coasts would be a familiar sight in an otherwise alien landscape. Of course one would not see the same coasts, the same rocks, the same grains of sand. They have long since gone, folded back into the belly of the planet by inexorable tectonic recycling, and replaced by new rock formations, risen during earthquakes, spilled from volcanic eruptions, or the uplifted compressed sediments of the ocean floor. The coasts themselves have changed, sea-levels have risen and fallen, new continents have formed, but the processes of coastal formation and erosion remain much the same. A coast today looks very much as it would have billions of years ago.

The grand time-scale of creation and destruction of the coast, of slow but continual movement of the coastline, is overlaid with a short-term rhythm that dominates all life there – the daily pattern of the tides. The gravitational forces of the moon and sun combined with the rotation of the earth result in a pattern of rising and falling waters around the world. In most areas the intertidal zone is covered twice per day by the ocean, and in between it is exposed to the atmosphere. The changing relative positions of sun and moon during the course of a month lead to a complicated pattern of tidal motion, including two very high and very low tides, the so-called 'spring' tides, when sun and moon are aligned and their gravitational effects are reinforced. About two weeks later 'neap' tides occur when moon and sun stand at right angles to each other, mitigating some of each others' gravitational forces. During neap tides the ocean is relatively calm and less ground is covered or exposed during the tides.

Geographic location has considerable influence on the amount of tidal movements. The Mediterranean Sea experiences only a metre or two difference between high and low tide – simply because the Mediterranean is almost completely landlocked. At the other end of the scale is the Bay of Fundy on the east coast of Canada, which has the world's largest tides with a difference of up to

17 metres. Oceanographers attribute the huge tidal range of the Bay of Fundy to a feedback effect called tidal resonance. The time a wave needs to travel from one side of the bay to the other and back again coincides exactly with the time between two tides. The result is somewhat comparable to the wave sloshing around in the bathtub when you move your body back and forth, trying to capsize the floating rubber duck. In extremely gently sloping areas like the Watten Sea off the Dutch and German North Sea coast the low tide retreats tens of kilometres at low tide, rendering dozens of islands temporarily landlocked – only to rush back in again a few hours later, reclaiming the muddy plains as sea floor.

This incessantly changing strip between low tide and high tide, the intertidal zone, poses huge challenges to any organism that tries to make a living here. Inhabitants of this environment often find themselves, quite literally, between a rock and a hard place.

The intertidal zone is a region of biological convergence – the inhabitants have either encroached from the sea or have edged in from the land. Life here must be especially hardy to deal with the dramatic cyclical changes in conditions. Organisms must contend with wide variations in temperature and salinity, with the risk of desiccation, and with fluctuating food supplies. To avoid these threats altogether, creatures that use the intertidal zone only when covered with water – such as many fish – retreat with the outgoing tide. Others, such as wading birds that feed when the intertidal area is exposed, do the opposite and retreat up the shore with the incoming tide. But the permanent residents must cope with the extremes that accompany the daily ebb and flow. Some dig themselves deep into moist sediments like lugworms, ghost shrimps and many bivalves. Others attach themselves to rocks by suction, glue or grappling hooks.

Intertidal plants show remarkable resilience to the extreme conditions. Seaweeds that grow high on rocky shores can lose up to 90 percent of their water contents and literally desiccate – only to rehydrate and revive again in the next incoming tide. Some terrestrial plants like cordgrass and glassworts or samphire have also invaded the intertidal zone and developed special mechanisms that either 'sweat out' the salt they are exposed to, or dilute it with fresh water accumulated in their thick fleshy stalks.

The physical form of coastline shapes the biological communities that live there. The most dramatic contrast is found between mudflats and rocky shores.

Mudflats are always areas with little wave action. They are found in estuaries and on very gently sloping coastlines. Very fine particles of sand or sediment are

deposited by rivers or by the incoming tides. The fine particles pack together closely, producing dense mud with very low oxygen concentrations – thus making breathing a big challenge. Most inhabitants of the mudflats burrow into the sediment to protect themselves from predators and the harsh and ever-changing conditions at the surface, but they use breathing siphons like snorkels above the ground to access the oxygen-rich water that comes in with the tide. The population of burrowing invertebrates in mudflats is tremendous and attracts numerous predators, from crabs and carnivorous worms to the wading birds that sift through the mud with their specialized beaks. These flocks are usually the only outward sign of the astonishing productivity of the mudflats.

Birds are particularly well suited to exploit the rich pickings of this niche – being on the wing has distinct advantages when one has to retreat from swift incoming waves and breaking surf. Hundreds of millions of wading birds congregate at low tide in mudflats and estuaries around the world, as well as along sandy coastlines. With specialized elongated beaks that resemble anything from tweezers to spoons, they sift through sediments rich in worms, clams and other burrowing invertebrates.

In the warmer regions of the planet a small group of unrelated terrestrial trees and shrubs called mangroves has specialized to live on the mud. Mangroves have found a solution to the problem of low oxygen content in the sediments and the high salinity of the seawater in which they are regularly bathed. Instead of taking up oxygen through the root system like other terrestrial plants, they have developed special 'air-roots' above the ground that are able to extract oxygen from the water or from the air, depending upon the tide level. Mangroves have also evolved specialized pores on their leaves to 'sweat out' the excess salt absorbed through their root system.

Mangrove forests are moody places with a dull colour palette, but they are just as important for the tropical coast as the much more flamboyant coral reefs. They act as important physical buffers between the forces of the ocean and the shoreline, counteracting coastal erosion. Their extensive root systems provide crucial nurseries for many fish species and offer a great home for encrusting animals like barnacles and sponges. Thus armoured, mangroves are protected from the damaging activities of shipworms and other boring intruders.

On rocky coastlines the very bones of the earth are exposed directly to the onslaught of the swirling ocean. Rocky shores represent the opposite extreme to mudflats. Rather than depositing material, the sea is eroding the shore-line with great force, smashing and grinding rock into rubble, pebbles, sand. A typical feature of all rocky shores is a distinct zonation of the species that live permanently attached to the rock. The upper end of each zone is determined by the degree of exposure to air and solar radiation that these organisms can

tolerate. The lower end is defined by predator pressure and competition.

As the surf breaks on the hard rocks it sends plumes of spray high into the air. This constant exposure to salt spray in the splash zone above the high tide mark makes it extremely difficult for most terrestrial organisms to cope. Some hardy terrestrial lichens have successfully invaded the splash zone, but it is mainly the encrusting marine invertebrates that dominate this area on the rocky shore. Exposed to the air and huge temperature differences twice a day, some hard-shelled invertebrates like mussels, limpets and barnacles protect themselves from drying out with tightly closing shells that trap water inside when the tide goes out. Crafty holdfast systems prevent them from being washed off the rock by crashing waves. Barnacles have developed a glue that is superior to the very best commercial glues, and mussels use strong protein fibres for the same purpose. Mobile molluscs such as limpets use a muscular foot as a suction cup to hold on to the rock. Other inhabitants of the tidal zone, such as crabs, rely on their mobility and move up and down the rock face in step with the tides.

Sea birds make good use of the steep and inaccessible cliff-faces of rocky shores above the high tide mark, with many species coming to land for the sole purpose of breeding. They aggregate in often huge and dense colonies, sometimes on precariously small ledges high above the roaring sea. Here they are safe from most predators yet close to the ocean's plentiful riches.

As the tide recedes from a rocky shore, natural hollows and crevices retain some of the seawater, producing a very special habitat. These rock pools provide havens for marine creatures that cannot survive outside the water for long. But they have to be tolerant of fluctuations in temperature and salinity – the water in these little pools can warm up or cool down considerably during the time they are cut off from the ocean. Likewise rain and the searing heat of the sun affect the salt content of the pool, which may range from almost pure freshwater to brine

Life between tides

0 m

10 m

As long as there have been oceans, there have been beaches. To our eyes beaches are usually beautiful, tranquil havens, but carving out a living in the intertidal zone is one of the planet's greatest challenges. Exposure to air, extreme temperature variations, changes in salinity, and the absence of a firm substrate make the sandy ocean beach a place where only the hardiest can survive.

Hooker's sea lion

0 m

Phocarctos hookeri
Size: 3 metres

300 m

A deep diver amongst marine mammals and one of the rarest sea lions in the world, Hooker's sea lions have been found diving as deep as 600 metres, although they usually hunt for fish and squid in shallow seas. Hauling out onto a beach after a day out at sea, this curious pup has only been independent of its mother for a few months.

Dusky dolphins

0 m
100 m

Lagenorhynchus obscurus
Size: 1.8 metres

A pod of dusky dolphins swims through clear waters. This species commutes between shallow coastal seas and oceanic waters in search of fishes and squid. Dusky dolphins prefer company and are usually found in small groups, though larger congregations of up to 500 individuals sometimes occur. Working together, they herd schools of fish towards the surface where they are easily picked off.

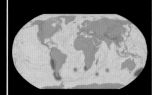

Australasian gannets

0 m

200 m

Morus serrator
Size: 85 centimetres

Affectionally cleaning each other's neck feathers is part of the bonding display between gannets when returning to the breeding colony. Gannets are at home in the air, on land and underwater. They are specialized dive-bombers that hit the surface of the ocean with speeds in excess of 100 kilometres per hour in pursuit of fish up to several metres below the waves.

Green turtle

0 m
— 1000 m

Chelonia mydas
Size: 1.5 metres

One of the larger marine turtles, the heaviest ever recorded green turtle weighed 395 kilograms (871 lbs). The thin stream of bubbles emanating from this green turtle's mouth signals the air-breathing, terrestrial origin of these reptiles. They spend most of their time at sea but females must still return to land to lay their eggs — which are buried on sandy beaches.

Turtle hatchlings

0 m

Chelonia mydas
Size: 5 centimetres

A mad rush for the ocean. Guided by the influence of the Moon and the reflection of the Sun on the water, these green turtle hatchlings are in a hurry to escape a multitude of predators, from seagulls to crabs, eager for an easy meal. But there is safety in numbers. Synchronized mass hatching ensures some of the turtles

Mangroves

0 m

Primordial-looking mangroves have been around since the days of the dinosaurs,
linking the ocean and the terrestrial world. Despite their ancient roots they
remain the only flowering plants except for seagrass that have managed to
re-invade the marine environment. They provide shelter for many invertebrate

Mudskipper

0 m

30 m

Periophthalmus kalolo
Size: 5 centimetres

Every time a mudskipper emerges from the sea and uses its strong pectoral fins to hop along the exposed mangrove mud, it is re-enacting a crucial step in the evolution of higher vertebrates – the conquest of the land. In fact, the mudskipper spends more time on land than underwater and many aspects of its physiology are better adapted to a terrestrial rather than aquatic lifestyle.

Saltwater crocodile

0m
30 m

Crocodylus porosus
Size: 5 metres

Saltwater crocodiles have changed little over hundreds of millions of years. Among the heaviest living reptiles, they can weigh over a ton and measure up to 6 metres in length – truly a force to be reckoned with. This sub-adult has been evicted from the freshwater breeding areas by territorial males and has to be content as the top predator in the coastal mangroves.

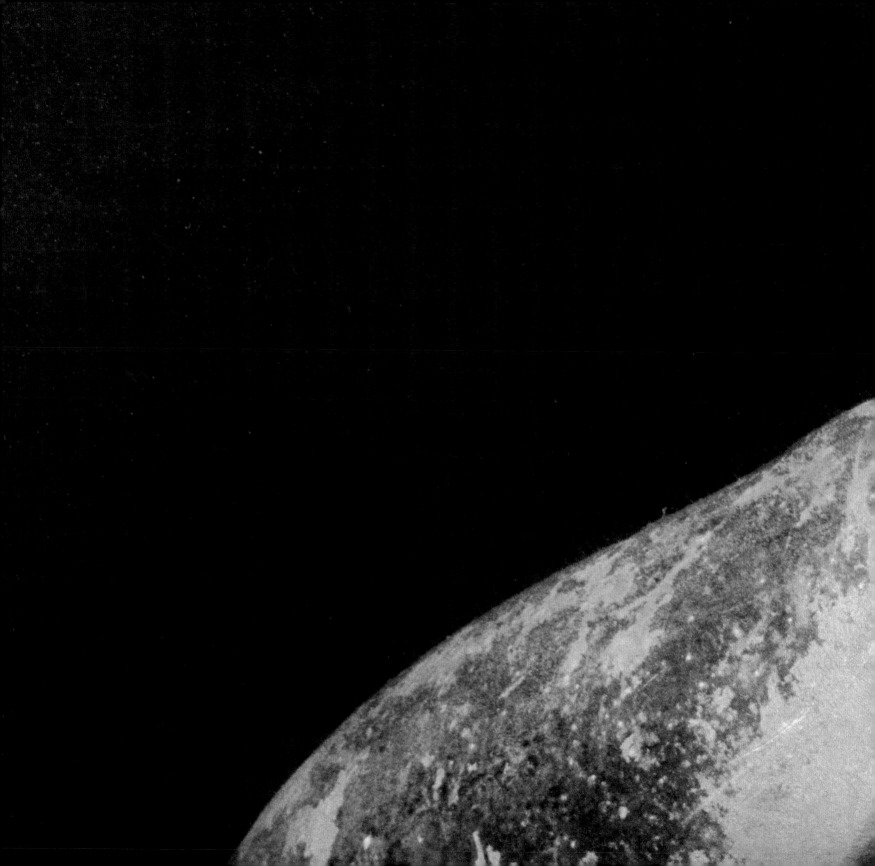

Sand flounder

0 m

-30 m

Rhombosolea plebeia
Size: 30 centimetres

Adult flounders are masters of disguise, both in terms of body shape and
cryptic coloration. A juvenile flounder looks much like any other fish, but
as it matures, one eye migrates to the other side of its head, while the body
transforms into the typical flattened shape, enabling it to lie on its side
and hide in the sand with both eyes standing proud of the sediment.

Starfish tubefeet

0 m

Coscinasterias muricata

Size: 20 centimetres

Like an alien machine, a starfish crawls along on scores of hydraulically powered tube feet. Starfish are among the ocean floor's most ubiquitous predators, using their powerful hydraulics to wrench open the shells of mussels and other bivalves, and then – in true horror-movie style – squeeze their

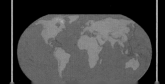

Rocky shore

0 m

Between a rock and a hard place: a giant wave crashes over the top of a rock the size of a fifteen-storey building. Under the thunderous breaking waves, plants and animals alike are holding on for dear life, using ingenious attachment devices – suction cups, glues and grappling hooks – to cling to the rocks. Mussel glue can

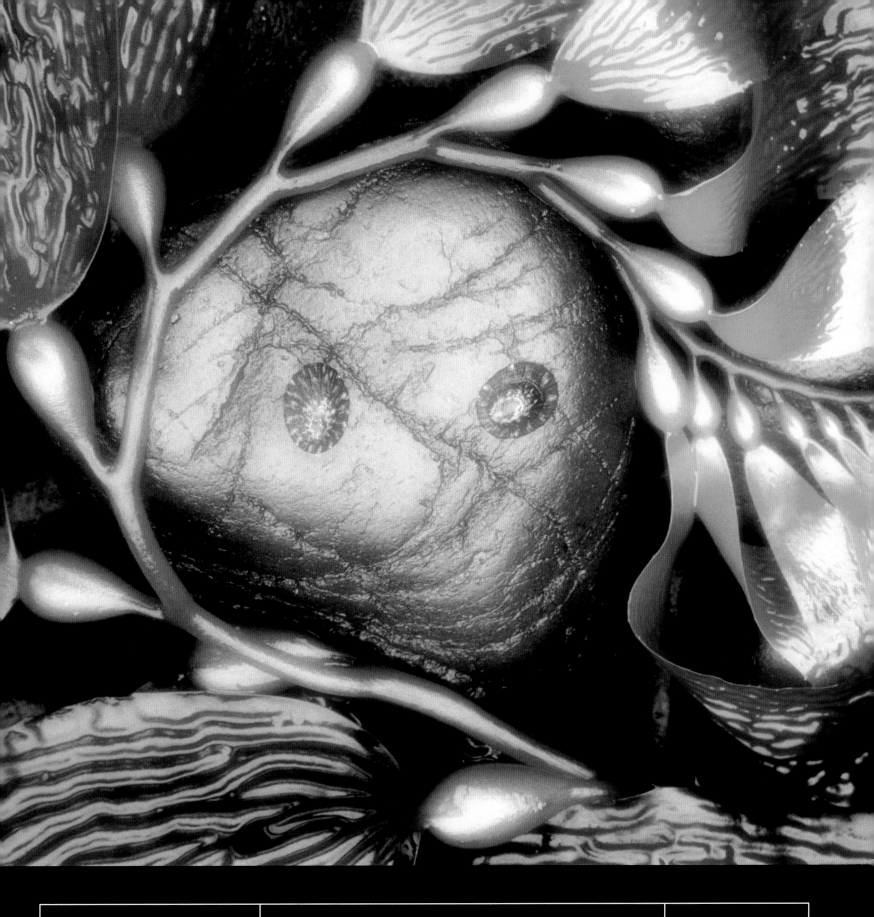

Radiate limpets

0 m

Cellana radians
Size: 2 cm

The tenacious limpet is a cousin of the sea snail. It attaches itself with a strong
suction foot to rocks in the intertidal zone, trapping some water in its shell when
the tide leaves it 'high and dry'. When submerged, the limpet moves in slow
motion from its home base, grazing algae off the adjacent rock surfaces. As the

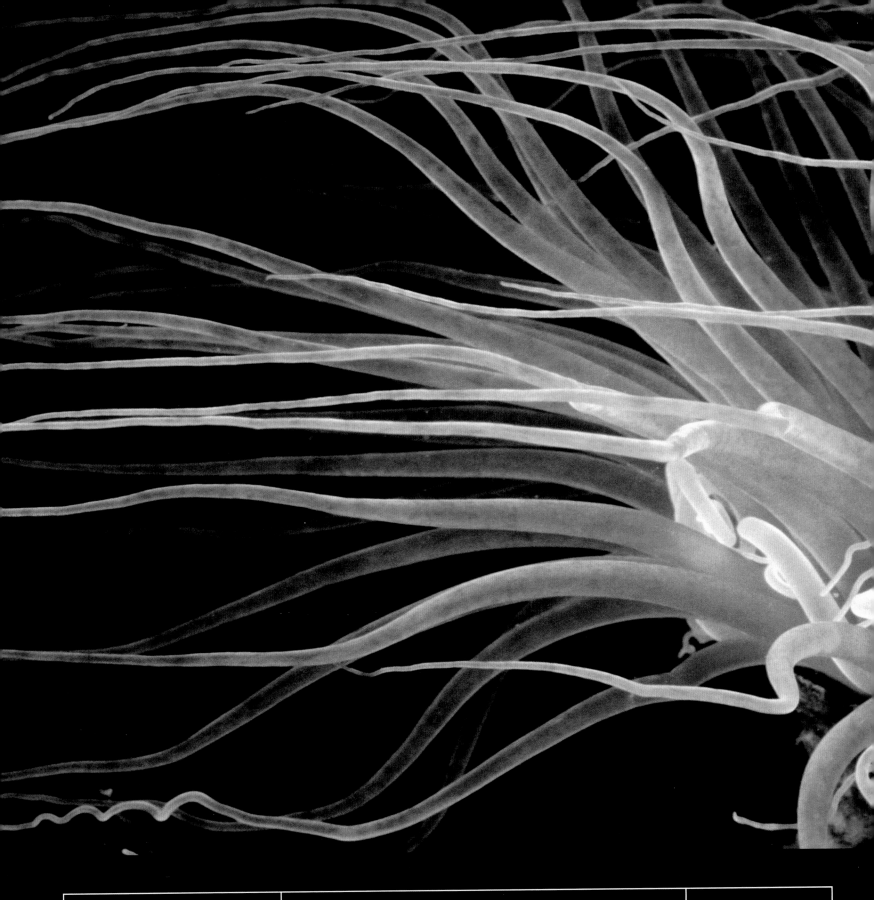

Tube anemones

Pachycerianthus
fimbriatus

Romantically named 'flowers of the sea', tube anemones are in reality predatory
animals that dig their holding foot deep into the sand to attach themselves to
rocks and other hard surfaces and ambush plankton with their stinging tentacles.
The tentacles then transport the catch into the mouth, at the centre of the 'flower',

2 Beneath the Tides

N THE SHALLOW WATERS below the low tide mark life is a lot easier than in the intertidal zone. Inhabitants of this subtidal zone don't have to cope with huge variations of temperature or salinity and they do not get exposed to air. At the same time there is still good access to sunlight and photo-synthesizing primary producers like algae and kelp can flourish. But just as in the exposed intertidal zone, the nature of the sea floor has a profound influence on the forms and shapes that life takes on beneath the tides.

Below sandy beaches and mudflats the subtidal zone is quite barren on the surface of the sea floor. The sediments are constantly shifting and give little opportunity for living things to settle down and establish a foothold. The few creatures that are visible on the shallow sandy sea floor are mostly suspension feeders like anemones or corals that hold their tentacles into the current to catch plankton and organic particles. The mobile inhabitants that live exposed on top of the sediments like shrimps and flatfish use elaborate body designs and colour schemes as camouflage.

Just like in the intertidal zone extremely high productivity can be found below the surface of the sea floor where burrowing clams hide from view exposing only their inhaling siphon to filter plankton. Densities of these clams can reach a staggering 500 individuals per square metre. Worms too make a living here by feeding on detritus, dead organic material, that sinks to the bottom and becomes part of the sediment. Predatory fish have specialized sensory systems that help them locate this hidden smorgasbord. Cod and catfish use barbels, touch-sensitive feelers around their mouth, to probe the sediment and locate the hidden prey. Stingrays use an even more sophisticated system for the same purpose – an electromagnetic sensor system capable of detecting the electric fields produced by living organisms.

The relative lack of observable life off sandy shores is more than counteracted by an abundance of visible life on rocky shores in cool and temperate regions

sea floor. That is the reason why they can only exist along rocky shores. Each plant has a holdfast that keeps it anchored to rocks on the seabed, and leaf-like fronds to photosynthesize and collect nutrients from the water column. The fronds have gas-filled chambers, or in some species separate gas-filled bladders, that provide buoyancy like a gas-filled balloon and maintain an upright position in the water column – thus maximizing exposure to sunlight.

The kelps are one of the ocean's primary producers, the foundation of a food chain, keystone organisms that provide a unique habitat for a huge community of associated organisms. Just as in land-based plants it is the ability of these algae to capture the sunlight and transform its energy into living tissue through photosynthesis that makes them so important. Like its terrestrial counterpart a kelp forest presents a cathedral-like serenity with shafts of light penetrating the cool dark shadows. Every inch here is filled with life. This intricate three-dimensional world offers a myriad of hiding places and anchor points, and supports a large community of herbivores and predators. Grazing urchins can have a huge impact on kelp communities, sometimes gnawing through the stalk and setting the whole plant adrift – thereby condemning it to death. A healthy kelp forest needs active predators to hold the grazing hordes in check. On the North American Pacific coast it is primarily the sea otters that repress the number of urchins. When the sea otter numbers decline, as happened in Alaska after the *Exxon Valdez* oil spill, the urchin population may explode and graze down entire forests of kelp before they themselves run out of food and diminish, in turn allowing recovery of the kelp.

The abundance of life on rocky shores continues down into deeper water until the continental shelf drops off into the deep sea. Even when the light fades and photosynthesis is no longer possible there are rich communities of rock-clinging organisms. Many of them look like plants – they have frond-like structures for feeding – but only animals can exist down here. And they are beautiful. When

ABOVE *A solitary squat lobster (*Munida gregaria*). In the shallow waters of the southern hemisphere these crustaceans can form shoals so vast, so dense they colour the sea red. Such numerical exuberance comes at a price however, and the squat lobster's list of predators is long – they are an important prey animal for many seabirds, marine mammals and fish.*

trap food particles before the water is expelled again through exit channels on the top of the animal. Barnacles use modified legs that they stretch out like a dip net to scoop up particles. Polyps and anemones seem more choosy, targeting individual plankton with their tentacles, whereas tubeworms use a feathery fan around their mouth like a drift net to catch all sorts of planktonic organisms. Colourful soft corals and anemones dominate the communities of these deeper-

lying slopes. They can form huge colonies by just budding off more polyps, creating evermore hungry mouths eager to ensnare plankton and detritus. The nutrients are then shared with the rest of the colony since all its polyps are connected by fluid channels.

The rich populations of filtering organisms on these slopes also attract predators. There are squadrons of urchins and starfish walking and preying on these rich pastures like grazing herds of cattle. Fish hide between the rocks and nibble here and there more selectively. They in turn are stalked by larger fish, and by marine mammals like seals and dolphins that move through and have their pick.

The shallow waters on rocky shores in tropical regions have a different, quite special, community on offer. In fact these communities are the crown jewels amongst the inshore environments of the ocean. As such they warrant their very own chapter – coral reefs.

Kelp forest

0 m

30 m

Macrocystis pyrifera
Size: 20 metres

Giant kelp is the fastest-growing plant in the sea, and perhaps the fastest in the world. When conditions are right, this kelp can grow an amazing 60 centimetres per day, building the foundations of one of the most productive and dynamic ecosystems of the planet. Every year we harvest about 100,000 tons of kelp to extract ingredients for the manufacture of ice-cream, toothpaste and jelly.

Garibaldi

0 m

Hypsypops rubicundus

Size: 30 centimetres

Named for an Italian general whose soldiers wore red, the garibaldi is a rare flash of exuberant colour amongst the subdued tones of the Californian kelp forest. It is also the loudest fish in the forest, producing a thump-like beat when threatened. Like most damselfish, the garibaldi is an attentive parent. The males

Steller sea lion

0 m

Eumetopias jubatus
Size: 2.5 metres

A curious young Steller sea lion explores its environment. Later in life, this innate curiosity will be rewarded with a rich and diverse diet that includes worms, snails, urchins and a wide variety of fish. Adult males grow to a more than a ton, and these northern Pacific giants roam from Japan to Alaska.

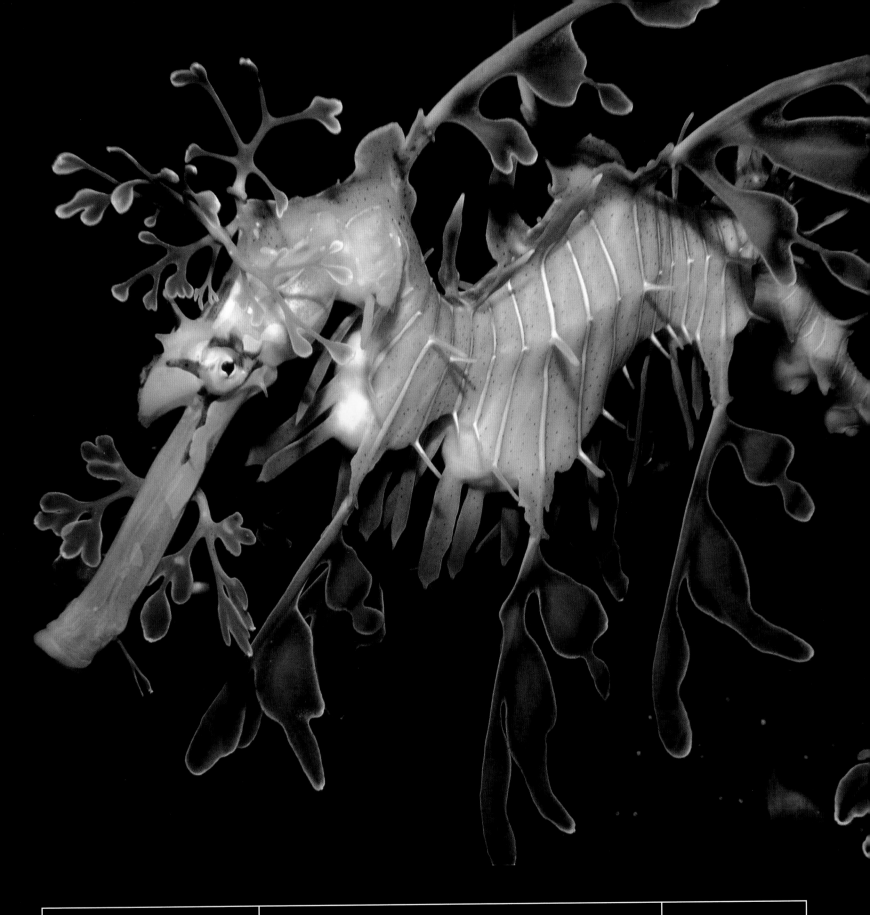

Leafy seadragon

0 m

Phycodurus eques

Size: 45 centimetres

Closely related to sea horses the leafy seadragon sports a perfect camouflage for its seaweed home. The rippling of tiny transparent fins propels these stealthy predators towards prey. None of the leafy appendages are used for locomotion, they just waft in the current like real seaweed. Plankton, unaware of the threat,

Broadclub cuttlefish

0m

30 m

Sepia latimanus
Size: 70 centimetres

Usually solitary, cuttlefish become sociable during the breeding season, culminating in a mating frenzy and egg-laying on the sea floor. Some males – the 'weedy nerds' of the cuttlefish community – go to extraordinary lengths for a chance to stealthily fertilize a female, going as far as even mimicking the colour patterns of the other sex to avoid incurring the wrath of alpha males.

Diadema urchin

0 m

Diadema palmeri
Size: 20 centimetres

~30 m

Atop an undersea pinnacle, a firebrick seastar and a pair of diadema urchins inhabit prime real estate amid dense schools of maomao. With tiny barbs on their needle-like spines, the urchins pose a challenge for any predator brave enough to attack these nocturnal grazers. Unwary human divers who get too close also face an agonizing experience.

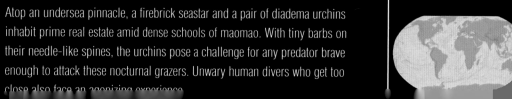

Rockwall community

┌ 0 m

Deep on the rocky reef, where there is not enough light for photo-
synthesizing seaweeds, gardens of plant-like animals make their living by
straining the passing water for plankton. Sponges dominate here. At their
best, the rock wall communities of temperate seas are more colourful than

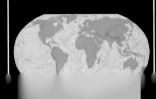

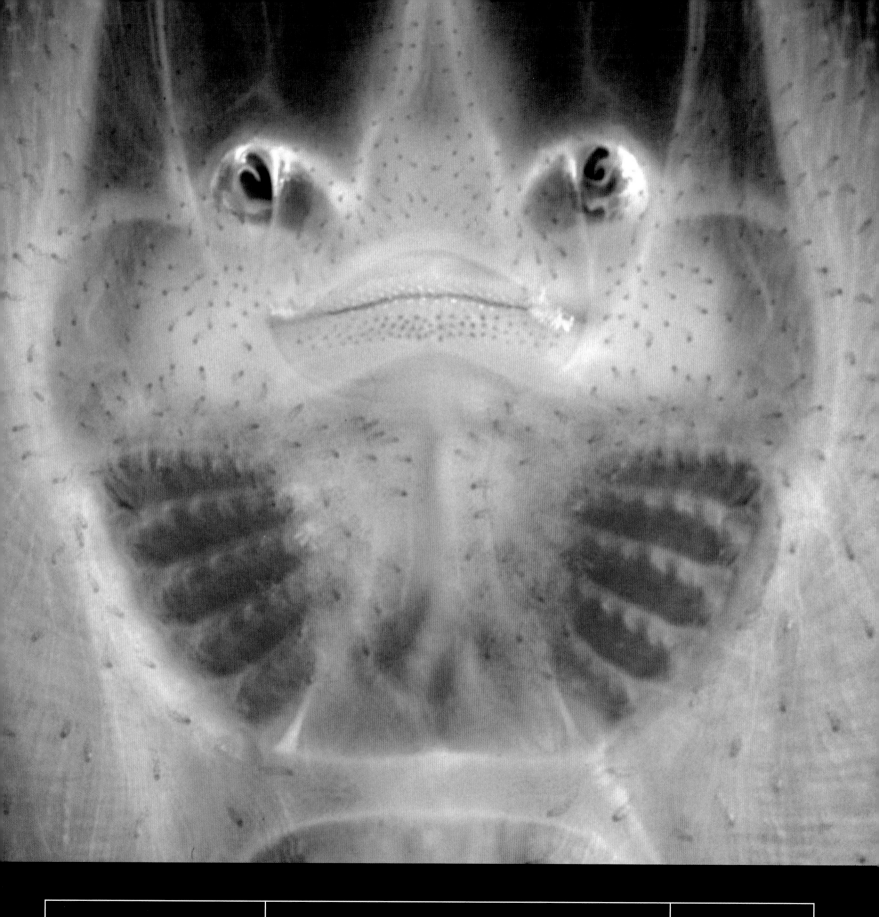

New Zealand rough skate

0 m

Dipturus nasutus

Size: 1 metre

A close encounter of the third kind? The 'eyes' in the face of a newborn New Zealand rough skate are in fact its nostrils. The translucent skin of this fish reveals the delicate architecture of the underlying cartilage skeleton, a structure it shares with all members of the shark and ray family.

Sea pen

Pteroeides bollonsi
Size: 20 centimetres

Unusual members of the coral family, sea pens anchor themselves on the sandy bottom and feed on zooplankton that passes by on the current. Sea pens are composed of a colony of polyps, with a large one making up the stem and several others forming feathery feeding branches. When touched, strobes of

Big-bellied seahorse

0 m

>30 m

Hippocampus
abdominalis

Size: 25 centimetres

Usually found only at great depth, in the inky waters of New Zealand's Fiordland
black coral trees occur close to the surface. Covered in a white layer of living
polyps, this tree shelters a big-bellied seahorse. In all seahorses it is the males
that fall pregnant, by gathering the fertilized eggs in a specialized belly pouch and
brooding them until the offspring are ready to be released into the open water

Squat lobsters

0 m

>30 m

Munida gregaria
Size: 5 centimetres

These squat lobsters have recently settled on the sea floor after a pelagic existence in the water column. Seasonal influxes of juvenile munida invade coastal waters in vast swarms of billions of individuals and provide a nourishing feast for aquatic species of all kinds, including whales and seabirds. After settling on the sea floor their communal nature gives way to fierce territoriality.

Tassled scorpionfish

Scorpaenopsis oxycephala
Size: 30 centimetres

The tassels on its chin, together with the mottled colouring, are part of this predator's strategy of lying in ambush until a small fish or unsuspecting crustacean swims within reach. The scorpionfish then lunges forward with surprising speed to engulf the prey with its huge mouth. While it lies in wait, 12 poisonous dorsal spines protect the scorpionfish from larger predators.

Juvenile striped catfish

0 m

>30 m

Plotosus lineatus
Size: 10 centimetres

Juvenile striped catfish form tight schools where the siblings literally stay in touch with each other, an unusual behaviour in schooling fish. Their bond is based on chemical cues that they pick up from the mucus on each other's skin. Bottom-dwelling catfish also have a delicate sense of touch and use long thin chin barbels to detect prey hidden under the sand.

Giant electric ray

0 m

Narcine entemedor

Size: 70 centimetres

Called numb fish in the ancient world, the Greek word for these rays – 'narce' – is the root for our 'narcotic'. No wonder, electric rays can produce charges of up to 220 volts, enough to knock an adult human to the ground. They produce their electric charges in organs on both sides of the head and use them to sense and

3 Coral Reefs

OVERFLOWING WITH AN ABUNDANCE OF COLOUR and beautiful life forms, tropical coral reefs are the most glamorous environments of the ocean. To us they represent the archetype of an underwater paradise, the warm crystal clear waters inviting snorkelling and scuba diving.

And indeed coral reefs are the most complex and diverse environment in the ocean. Their equivalent on land would be an old and mature rainforest. And like the rainforest it is the coral reef itself that is alive. It is built completely by living organisms related to sea anemones – the coral polyps. Over thousands of years colonies of these tiny animals excreted minute exoskeletons of limestone that slowly built up the reef. Billions of polyps form a living outer skin on the surface of the coral mass. Growing on the skeletons of their ancestors, these polyps extrude their tiny tentacles at night to trap drifting microscopic food.

Like the kelp forests on temperate rocky shores, reef-building corals are keystone organisms around which an entire ecosystem develops. Contrary to popular belief, the vibrant blue ocean of the tropics is almost devoid of life. The warm surface water acts like a lid on a pot and traps nutrient-rich water in the deep, out of reach for the primary producers like green algae that rely on sunlight to photosynthesize. The very fact that the water is blue indicates that it is poor in nutrients and plankton – rendering it a biological desert. Coral reefs represent oases in this desert, supporting an abundant diversity of life. Like an underwater city the reef provides shelter to its inhabitants that have to put up with cramped quarters in exchange for quick and easy access to food and mating opportunities.

The key to the success of tropical corals lies in their role in primary production. Coral polyps form a symbiotic relationship within their tissue with microscopic algae that convert sunlight into sugars – food for both the algae and their hosts. This alliance with the photosynthesizing algae gives the coral polyps the edge in the desert of tropical seas. Like astronauts with a life-support system they can colonize the barren rocks of the shallow tropical seas and turn them into flowering gardens. They can feed and grow ever-larger colonies as long as the water has the right temperature and they have plenty of sunshine, even when there are not many nutrients available in the water column – they can always fall back on to their microscopic 'backup generators'.

A coral reef develops on rocky shores and grows fastest in shallow sunny waters. First it forms a fringing reef, running like a band along the coastline or around an island. Over the years it continues to grow outwards from the coast

forming a lagoon in the process. The reef has turned into a barrier reef. If it is growing on a volcanic sea-mount that slowly sinks and disappears, then the last stage of its evolution will be an atoll, a ring of coral islands around a deep lagoon.

Corals are broken down to gravel and ultimately to sand by wave action and also by a variety of animals. The skeleton of the coral is dissolved by sponges, bored into by molluscs that look for a hiding space and chewed up by parrotfish that are after the living polyps, but, behaving a bit like a bull in a china shop, they simply break off sizeable chunks of coral including the limestone skeleton and eat the lot. The limestone actually helps the parrotfish's digestion by grinding up the living tissue of the coral and gets ultimately excreted as a trail of sand that rains back on to the reef. Accumulating coral sand forms sandbanks or even islands, called cays. It also becomes the substrate for seagrass meadows to grow, which are important tropical ocean habitats in their own right. Some of the sand grains continue to be ground down, until the limestone itself dissolves back into the seawater, providing a new generation of coral polyps with the resources to build their skeletons.

All coral reefs show distinct zonation patterns that are influenced by the location and the physical exposure to wave action and currents. The crest is the most exposed area of the reef. It is formed by the outer ridge and takes the full pounding of breaking oceanic waves. Only very few robust coral species can survive here, in fact this area is dominated by hardy red and flexible brown algae. The seaward slope below the crest extends down into deep water, where the community is most diverse. Big coral trees grow at a depth where light penetration is still good but below the battering of the waves at the top. This is the region where the big fish patrol the edge of the reef.

On the other side behind the crest is a shallow zone that is aptly named the reef flat. It is the backwater of the reef that is sheltered from the waves, but very exposed to the heat of the sun. Coral growth here is minimal and instead erosion becomes a significant factor. The shallow reef flat is dominated by green algae that thrive in the sheltered and sunny conditions. This algal turf is one of the most productive plant communities in the world, producing up to 5 kilograms of plant matter per square metre per year. No wonder then that there is an army of vegetarian fish and invertebrates that thrive on this bounty.

With herbivores come predators. Invertebrates like crabs and nudibranchs, anemones and cone snails together with predatory fish have developed many

Yellow soft coral

0 m

Dendronephtya sp.

Size: 1 metre

Soft corals lack a calcifying skeleton and don't actually contribute to the building of the reef. Despite its enormous size this coral tree feeds almost exclusively on small phytoplankton, since it lacks the strong stinging cells that are needed to stun and catch the more active zooplankton.

Brittle stars

```
┌ 0 m
│
│
└ 30 m
```

Ophiothela danae
Size: 2 centimetres

The yellow arms of tiny brittle stars, cousins of starfish, cling tenaciously to
the vivid red branch of a fan coral. The exact nature of this relationship is
unknown, but observations of other species have shown that brittle stars remove
smothering detritus from their hosts, making their presence on the coral's
branches beneficial for both partners.

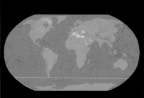

Crown of thorns

0 m

30 m

Acanthaster planci
Size: 25 centimetres

A voracious feeder of living coral tissue, this venomous starfish has been
blamed for much of the damage that has occurred on tropical reefs in recent
years. However, these starfish have always played their part in the reef ecosystem
and were once kept in check by a few specialized predators like the giant triton,
a beautiful sea snail that has since been over-harvested by humans.

Yellowback fusiliers

```
┌ 0 m



└ 30 m
```

Caesio teres
Size: 40 centimetres

Very fast swimming plankton hunters with streamlined bodies, fusiliers form large schools over the reef seeking safety in numbers from predators. The colour contrast between their yellow tails and bluish bodies is a dazzling form of camouflage, helping visually to break up the fusiliers' body contours, confusing any predator that may attack.

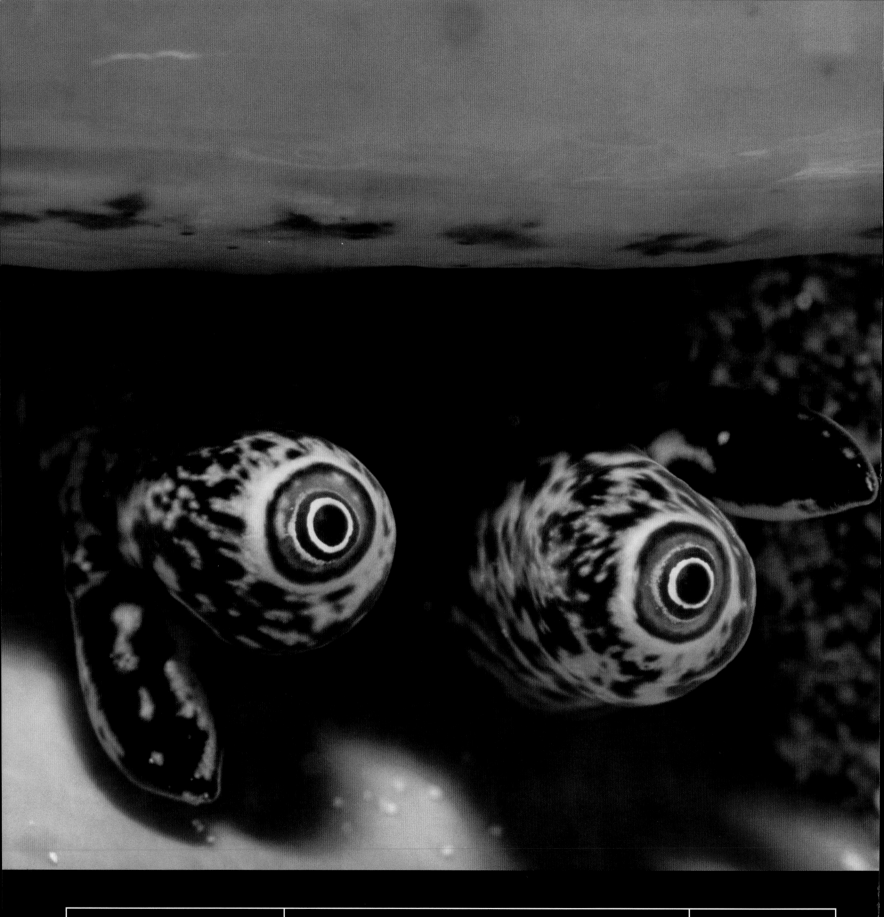

Queen conch

0 m
30 m

Eustrombus gigas
Size: 30 centimetres

A queen conch peeks out from its shell. This marine snail carries its eyes on long stalks and even has a special notch in the rim of its shell that allows its 'periscopes' to have a good look around without exposing the vulnerable body to predators. At 30 centimetres long, it is the largest marine snail in North America.

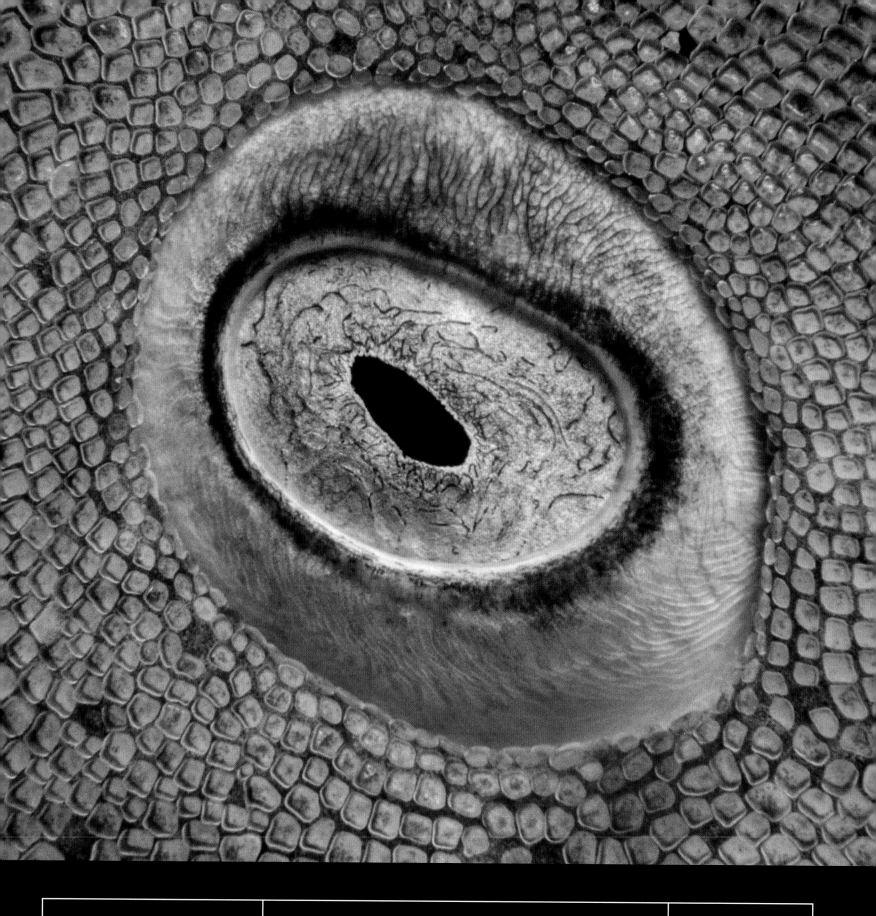

Tawny nurse shark

0 m

Nebrius ferrugineus
Size: 3 metres

30 m

Sharks had a reputation of being half blind – but the opposite is true, they have rather sophisticated eyes. Most fish have a fixed pupil that cannot adjust to different light conditions, but sharks have an adjustable pupil just like us. Sharks, like cats, also have a reflective layer at the back of the eye that collects and amplifies dim light, rendering their eyes up to ten times more sensitive than ours.

Great barracuda

0 m

Sphyraena barracuda

Size: 1.5 metres

Like incoming fighter planes a school of barracuda patrols the rim of the reef. Their razor-sharp teeth, resistance to many toxins and lightning speed put the barracuda firmly amongst the most fearsome predators of the reef. While the young fish hunt openly in schools like this, older fish are usually solitarily –

Grey reef shark

0 m

Carcharhinus amblyrhynchos
Size: 2.5 metres

—1000 m

Nomads of the reef, grey reef sharks are mostly active at night, but occasionally also form schools during the day, hunting for crabs and shrimps. They are quite inquisitive and may approach and investigate divers – sometimes showing a visual threat display with an overarched back and swimming with exaggerated movements.

Harlequin shrimp

0 m

Hymenocera picta
Size: 4 centimetres

30 m

The lovely colours of these harlequin shrimps are misleading – they are actually in the process of eating their prey alive. In a procedure that may take several weeks, these insatiable predators will turn a starfish on its back and slowly eat their hapless victim from the tips of its arms to its central disc. This keeps the starfish alive – and therefore fresh – while they consume it.

Mantis shrimp

scale

0 m

─ 30 m

Odontodactylus scyllarus
Size: 12 centimetres

Like a little alien with superpowers, the mantis shrimp is an almost unstoppable predator. It swings its hunting clubs with a speed that approaches that of a rifle bullet and can break aquarium glass. Additionally, its vision is unmatched in the animal kingdom. With ten different receptors it can not only detect colour, but also polarized light and can even perceive depth using only one eye.

Lionfish

┌ 0 m

└ >30 m

Pterois sp.

Size: 30 centimetres

A hunting red lionfish uses long wing-like fins and lightning-fast reflexes to herd its prey into a corner on the reef. Its spines are venomous and can inflict painful wounds to divers when touched. Lionfish are native to the Pacific, but have recently found their way into warm coastal waters of the eastern USA where they may pose a threat to the native fish stock.

Box jellyfish

0 m
>30 m

Chiropsalmus sp.
Size: 25 centimetres

Also known as sea wasps, box jellyfish are notorious threats to swimmers during the summer months in the tropical Indo-Pacific, where thousands of people have died after being stung. These jellyfish have a total of 24 eyes. On each corner of their body they carry a set of six eyes required to orientate themselves in the water column, and probably also to lock on to their prey.

Blue-ringed octopus

0 m

30 m

Hapalochlaena lunulata
Size: 10 centimetres

Just the size of a golf ball, the diminutive blue-ringed octopus is one of the deadliest animals in the world. With venom that is 10,000 times stronger than cyanide, and for which there exists no antidote, this creature is lethal to humans. Its famous blue rings become visible only when it is almost too late for the victim – when the octopus feels threatened and is about to attack.

Dog-faced pufferfish

0 m
30 m

Arothron nigropunctatus
Size: 12 centimetres

Although it contains the same poison as the blue ringed octopus (tetrodotoxin), the dog-faced pufferfish is toxic only when eaten. Prior to such a last-ditch defence, it will inflate itself by swallowing water when threatened. The pufferfish lives a predatory lifestyle using its fused teeth to crunch up the hard shells of snails and crustaceans, but sometimes it also grazes on algae.

Porcupine fish

```
 0 m
|
|
|
 30m
```

Diodon sp.
Size: 20 centimetres

Alarmed by the presence of a predator this porcupine fish inflates itself to double
its normal size, reducing the number of potential predators to those that have
a very big mouth (and a steel palate). It belongs to the same order as the
pufferfish, but carries additional spikes for defence. When the fish relaxes the
spikes all fold backwards making the porcupine fish more aqua-dynamic.

Banded sea krait

0 m

30 m

Laticauda colubrina
Size: 1.5 metres

With a left lung that runs almost the entire length of its body, this extremely poisonous sea snake can remain underwater for extended periods of time hunting for crabs and small fish. Unlike some sea snakes, banded sea kraits still have to return to land to lay their eggs, whereas some of their cousins are so attuned to their adopted marine habitat that they give birth at sea to live young.

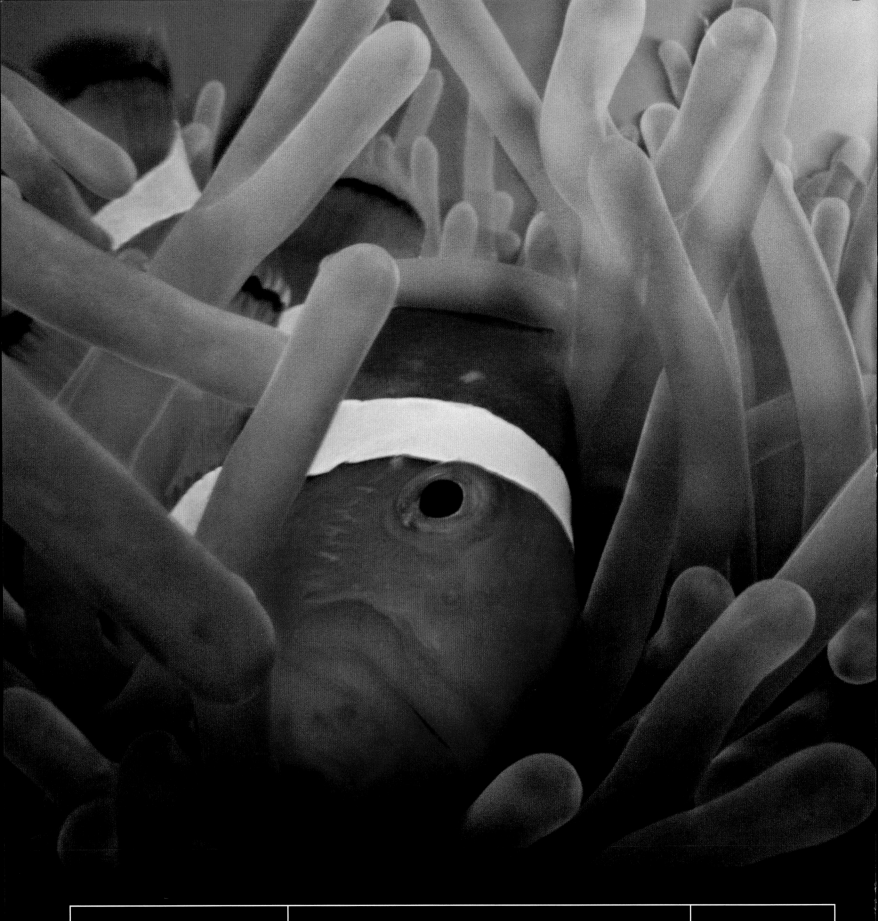

Clown anemonefish

0 m

30 m

Amphiprion ocellaris
Size: 6 centimetres

One of the best examples of symbiosis is the mutual relationship between the clown anemonefish and the anemone. The fish gains shelter and protection by living amongst the tentacles of its host anemone, shielded from predators that are not immune to the anemone's venom. For the anemone, the fish probably works like a decoy duck on a pond, luring in other fish that may become a meal.

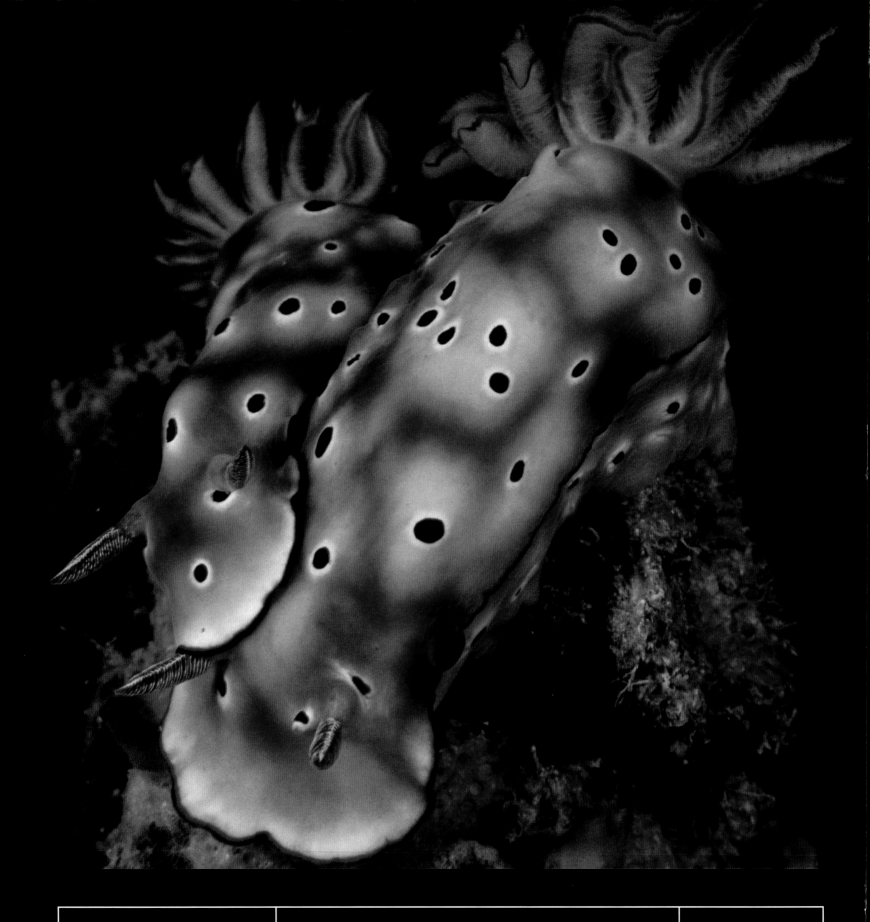

Sea-slugs

0 m

—30 m

Risbecia tryoni
Size: 6 centimetres

Sea-slugs or nudibranchs are among the most beautiful creatures in the ocean, a dramatic contrast to the subdued colours of their terrestrial kin. They carry frill-like gills on their back and announce with their vivid colours that they are not a good meal. Many of them are ferocious hunters that specialize in preying on toxic creatures and then retain their victims' poison for their own defence.

Hermit crab and anemones

0 m
30 m

Crab: Dardanus pedunculatus
Anemone: Calliactis sp.
Size: 12 centimetres

A symbiotic relationship has been forged between hermit crabs and anemones. With their stinging tentacles the anemones help the crab by scaring away predators. In return they get the leftovers from the crab's meals. A hermit crab will even transfer its anemones to a new shell when it has outgrown its old one – a clear case of keeping your friends close, and your anemones closer.

Galapagos sea lion

|— 0 m

Zalophus californianus wollebaeki
Size: 1.5 metres

|— 200 m

Inflating to double its normal size, a pufferfish tries desperately to discourage this mischievous Galapagos sea lion from eating it. However, since the pufferfish is indigestible, the sea lion is probably only interested in a playful encounter with a living 'ball'. In fact the skin of these fish is so highly toxic that such a meal would be a sea lion's last supper.

Potato grouper

0 m | Epinephelus tukula
Size: 2 metres

Growing up to two metres long, the Potato grouper is an ambush hunter that hides motionless behind chunks of coral until a suitable meal passes by. Then the seemingly cumbersome beast suddenly erupts into life, lunging forward with lightning speed and swallowing its prey in one gulp with its huge mouth.

Rockwall cave

0 m

Sunbeams stream down through the entrance of a large sea cave in Tonga with divers descending. Cliff faces on rocky shores continue into the inky depths far below the ocean surface. In the clear waters of the tropics, the rock walls provide a base for coral growth and hiding places for predators and prey alike.

Mimic octopus

0 m
30 m

Thaumoctopus mimicus
Size: 60 centimetres

Pretending to be a tropical flatfish, a mimicking octopus glides across the sea floor. Only discovered in 1998, the mimicking octopus's repertoire of impersonations also includes sea snakes and lionfish. The only known animals able to impersonate a variety of other species, their 'shape-shifting' ability greatly increases their chances of survival when faced by a predator.

Burrowing clam

0 m

−30 m

Tridacna squamosa
Size: 60 centimetres

Burrowing clams carry hundreds of tiny eyes along the brightly coloured edge of their mantle. The eyes are fairly primitive, but can detect shadows, triggering the mollusc to close its shell when threatened. Sensitive to ultraviolet and blue light, they also enable the clam to adopt an optimal position in relation to the sun, giving its symbiotic algae the best possible illumination for photosynthesis.

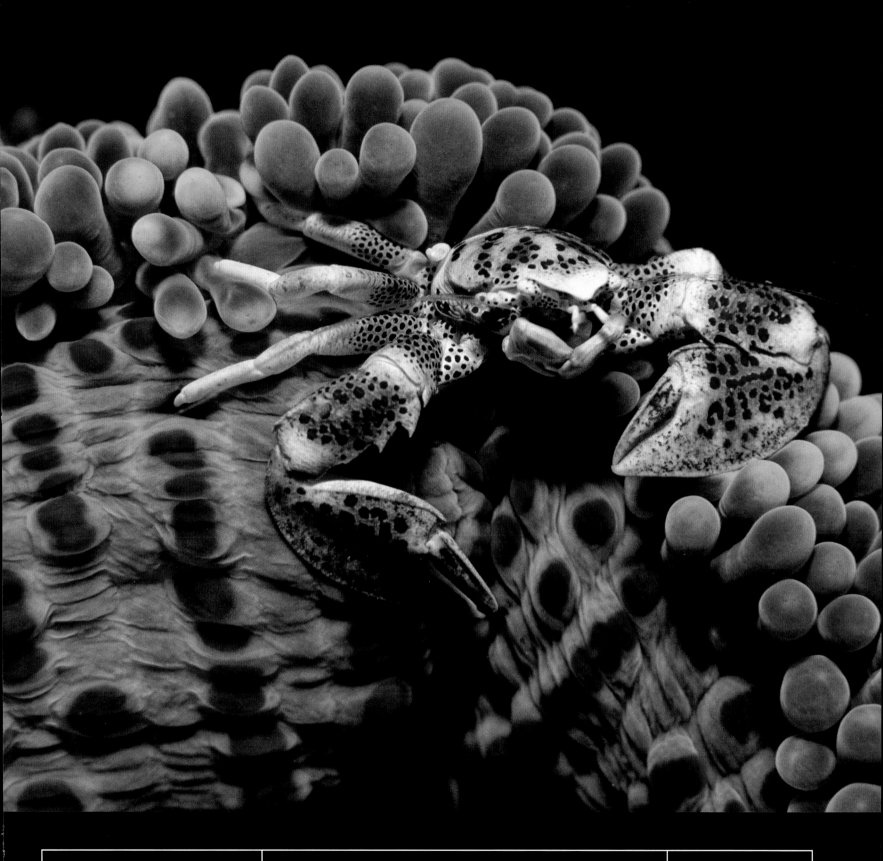

Porcelain crab

0 m

─30 m

Neopetrolisthes ohshimai
Size: 2.5 centimetres

Waving its claws, maybe in an effort to keep competing anemone fish from its home, a porcelain crab is hiding amongst the tentacles of its host anemone. Like the anemone fish, it is immune to the stinging cells of the anemone. The name is derived from its apparent fragility as it easily sheds limbs for distraction when attacked by a predator.

Pygmy seahorse

0 m
30 m

Hippocampus bargibanti
Size: 2 centimetres

Hidden amongst the branches of a Gorgonian coral lives the elusive pygmy seahorse. It is as small as your fingernail and has taken on the appearance of its host so perfectly that the first pygmy seahorse species was only found in 1970 – a reminder of the exciting discoveries that are still to be made beneath the waves.

Pygmy seahorse

⌐ 0 m

Hippocampus denise
Size: 2 centimetres

└ 30 m

Each species of pygmy seahorse has adapted over many generations to live upon just one particular coral. In addition to their almost perfect camouflage, the pygmy seahorse's sluggish movements even blend in with the natural swaying of its coral host. This species is found exclusively on the fan coral. Under 20 millimetres long, it is one of the smallest of all seahorses,

Pearlfish

0 m
30 m

Carapus sp
Size: 5 centimetres

In an exotic residential preference, the pearlfish lives within the digestive system of a sea cucumber during the day. Since sea cucumbers breathe through their anus, this provides an easy entry and exit point for the fish. At night the pearlfish leaves its protected refuge to feed on small crustaceans, although occasionally it will supplement its diet by nibbling on the gonads of its host.

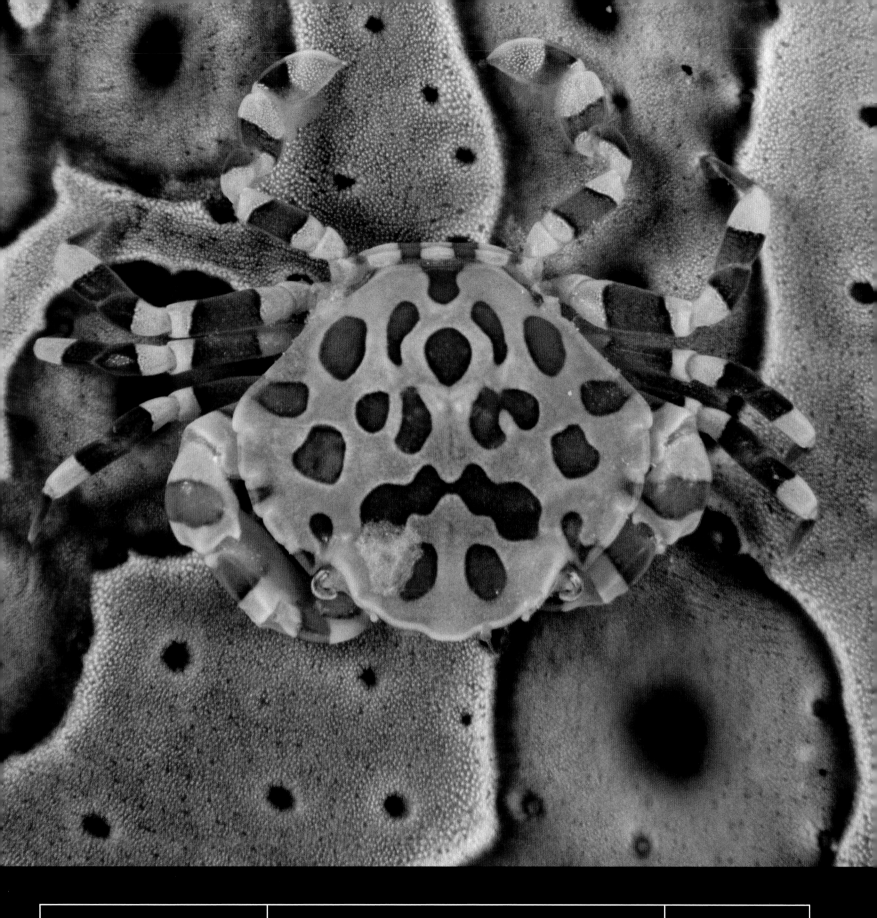

Sea cucumber crab

0 m
30 m

Lissocarcinus orbicularis
Size: 1 centimetre

Perfectly camouflaged, this tiny crab lives on the surface of a sea cucumber, feeding off food scraps left behind by its host. The sea cucumber doesn't benefit from the crab's presence, but neither is it harmed, making this one-sided relationship a commensal association, rather than a parasitic or symbiotic relationship.

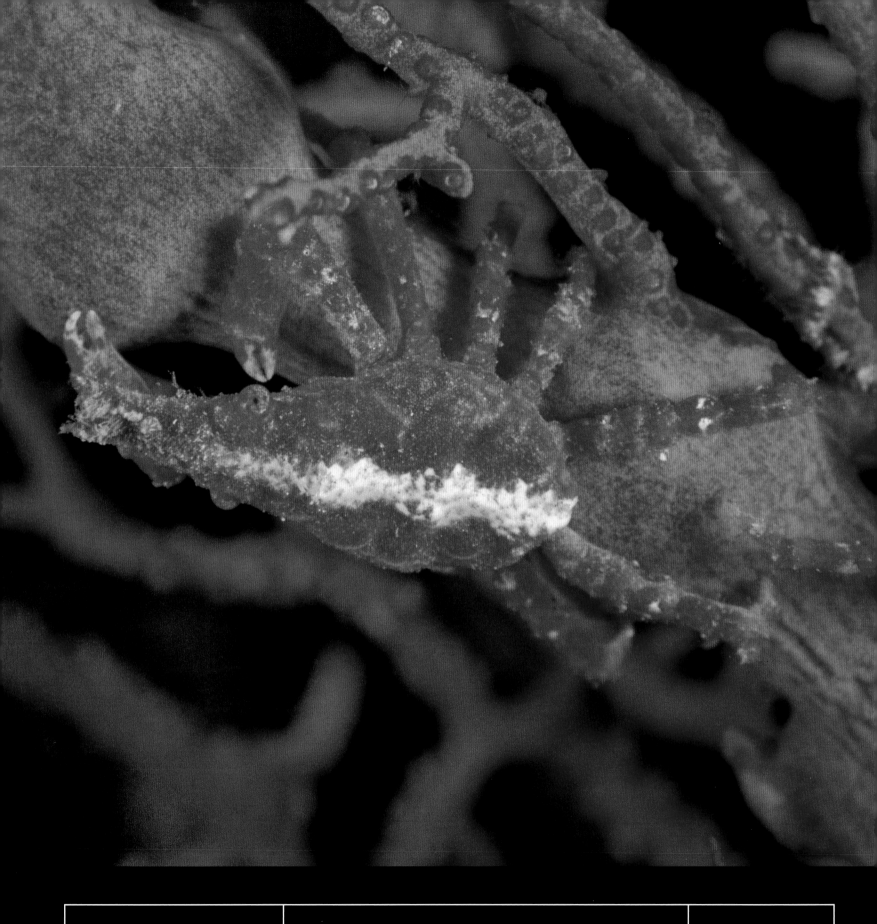

Spider crab

```
┌─0 m
│
│
└─30 m
```

Xenocarcinus conicus
Size: 1 centimetre

A magician in invisibility, the spider crab acts like an aquatic chameleon by matching its appearance to the background coral. Members of the same species come in many different disguises, each one being a perfect match in colour with the coral on which that particular individual lives. Sometimes they even decorate themselves with little bits taken off their host coral.

Razorfish

Aeoliscus strigatus
Size: 14 centimetres

A school of razorfishes hovers vertically amongst the branches of a red fan coral. This unusual orientation not only helps these bottom feeders in finding their next meal, it also doubles as protection from predators since it creates a seaweed-like appearance. Razorfish will also slide in amongst the long spines of diadema urchins for additional protection when predators threaten.

Plane wreck

┌ 0 m

└ — 8 m

Worlds are colliding off the coast of Papua New Guinea where the wreck of a
Second World War fighter plane has turned into an artificial reef – housing
and protecting a multitude of life. Such beneficial shelter is not needed by the
clown anemonefish, living happily in plain view, protected amongst the stinging
tentacles of their host.

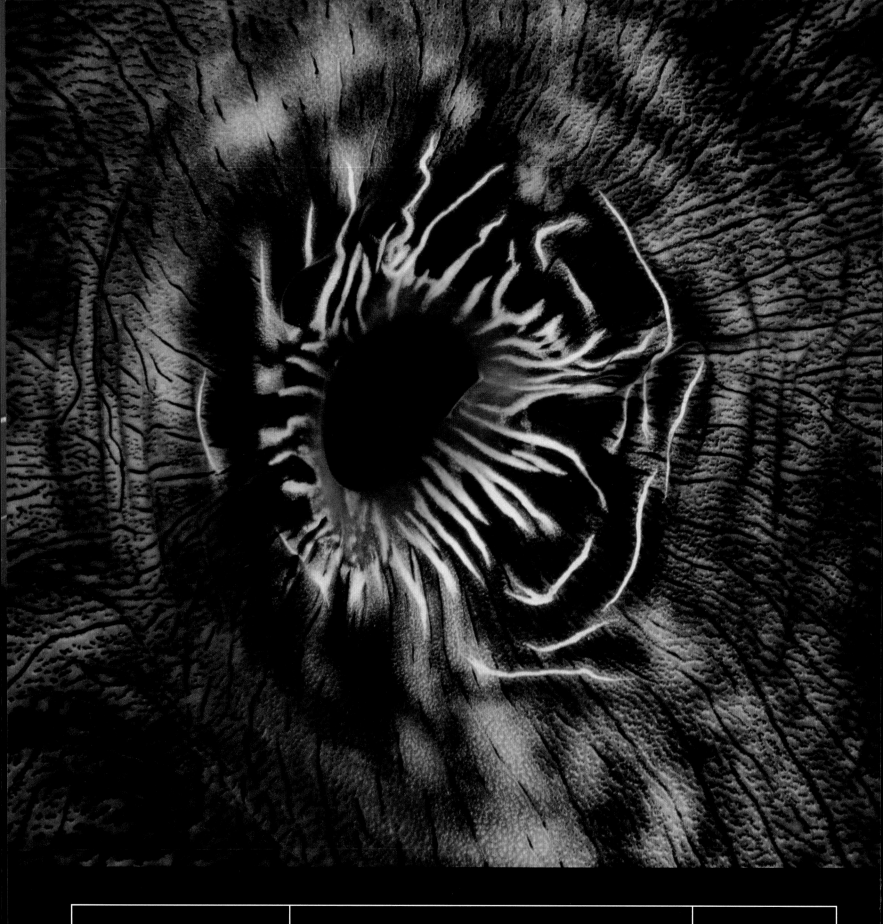

Giant clam

┌─0 m

└─30 m

Tridacna gigas
Size: 1.2 metres

This iridescent elephant's eye is actually the breathing siphon of a giant clam, the largest bivalve in the world. With a lifespan of over a century, giant clams may grow to more than a metre in length and weigh in excess of 200 kilograms. Just like the stony corals, they house symbiotic algae in their tissue, deriving much of their energy from these microscopic helpers.

Fluorescent coral

0 m

30 m

Blastomussa wellsi
Size: 10 centimetres

Under artificial light, coral polyps fluoresce – revealing the presence of natural sunscreen pigments. Corals equipped with these pigments cope better with the combined effects of global warming and high ultraviolet levels than those without. They appear less vulnerable to the 'bleaching' phenomenon that has devastated reefs throughout the world in recent years.

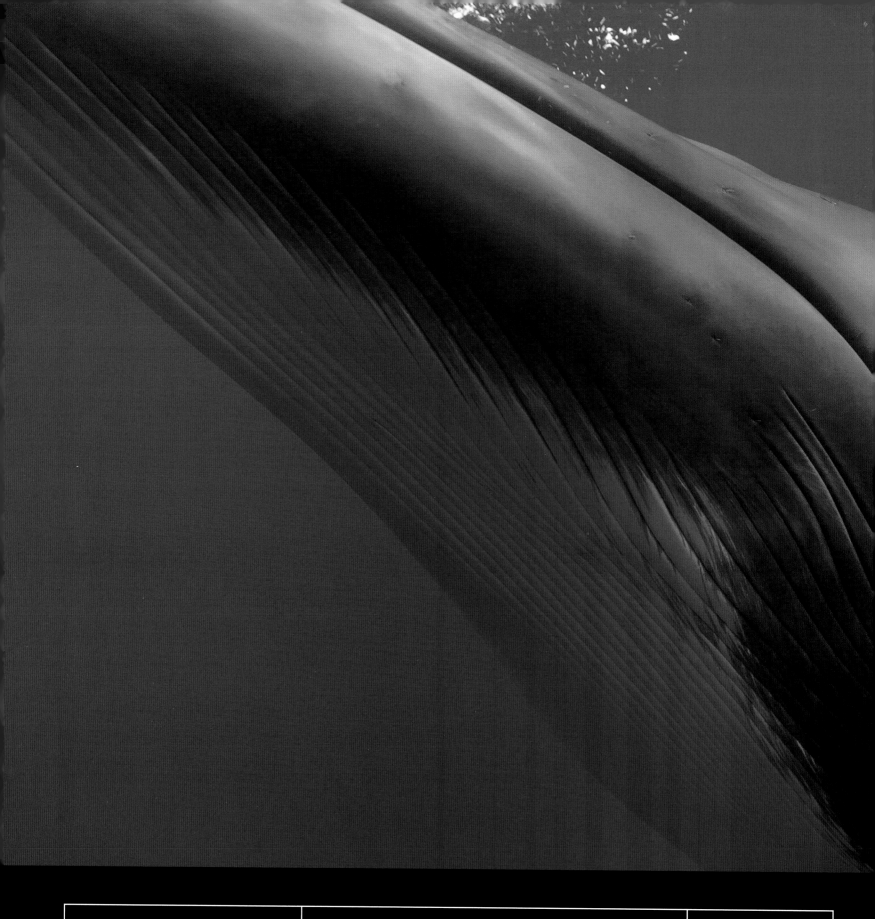

Dwarf Minke whale

0 m

Balaenoptera acutorostrata

Size: 8 metres

Innately curious, dwarf Minke whales often approach divers in the warm waters of the northern Great Barrier Reef. Named after an eighteenth-century Norwegian whaler known for hunting undersized whales, these diminutive whales grow eight metres long and migrate south into Antarctic waters to

Manta ray

0 m

Manta birostris
Size: 9 metres

200 m

Gliding through the deep blue with wings spanning up to nine metres, the manta is the largest of all rays. These plankton feeding giants are often accompanied by remora fish. Securely attached by an adhesive sucker, the remoras catch a free ride and enjoy access to a steady food supply. This manta has remoras attached to its belly and gill slits; their presence probably does the manta no harm.

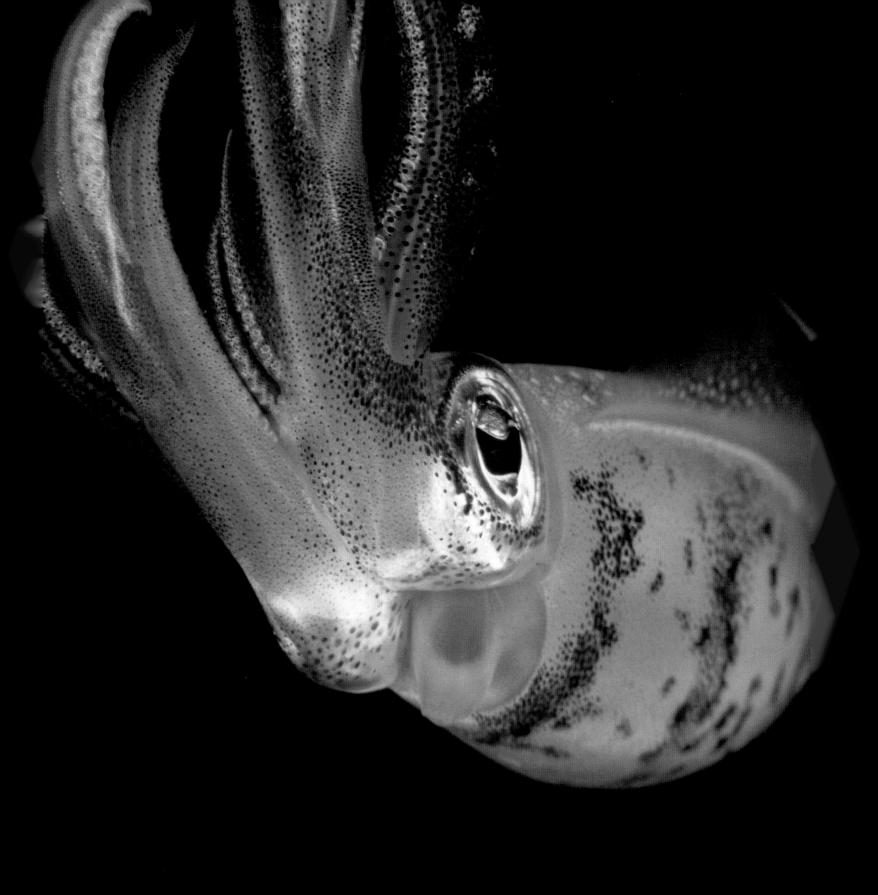

Bigfin reef squid

0 m
200 m

Sepioteuthis lessoniana
Size: 20 centimetres

During the day these large squid stay well offshore but by night they approach the reef edge in large schools to hunt for fish and shrimp. Like their octopus and cuttlefish cousins, squid have very well-developed eyesight and hunt visually. Two long tentacles shoot out to envelop their prey and bring it within reach of its arms and a parrot-like beak that tears the victim to bits.

Golden damselfish

0 m
30 m

Amblyglyphidodon aureus
Size: 7 centimetres

Aerating the hundreds of eggs attached to a whip coral, a golden damselfish guards his nest. Usually the male is responsible for caring for the eggs after spawning. During courtship he chooses a nest site and tries to attract a female by making loud chirping sounds. If another male damselfish dares to enter his territory he changes his tune and produces warning popping sounds.

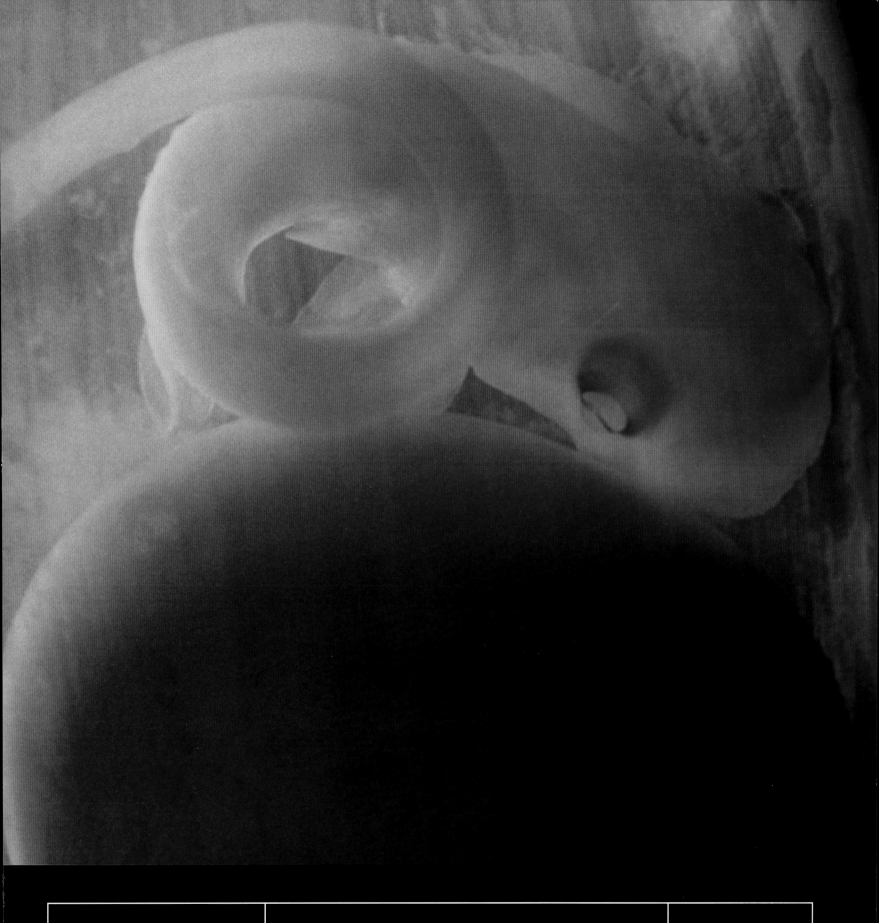

Swell shark egg

0 m
1000 m

Cephaloscyllium
ventriosum

Size: 90 centimetres

The swell shark embryo develops outside the mother's body in an egg case, also known as mermaid's purse. By contrast, hammerhead shark embryos develop within the mother and are born as small but fully developed sharks. Sand tiger sharks exhibit a more competitive, and somewhat grizzly, approach – routinely cannibalizing their unborn siblings while still inside the mother's uterus.

Opalescent inshore squid

0 m

>30 m

Loligo opalescens
Size: 20 centimetres

Vast schools of opalescent inshore squid congregate for an orgy of sex and death. Having attracted a mate with complex colour patterns and movements, the male uses a specialized arm to place a sperm packet in her mantle cavity. The females lay their fertilized eggs in clusters, forming beds that can cover acres of ocean floor. After mating the adults die and the new generation hatches three to five weeks later.

Giant barrel sponge

0 m

Xestospongia testudinaria
Size: 1 metre

30 m

Smoke pours from a living underwater chimney: timed by the lunar cycle, barrel sponges synchronize their spawning, releasing eggs and sperm en masse. The ensuing milky cloud drifts over the coral reef, absolutely overwhelming predators, and greatly increases the chances of successful fertilization of the eggs.

4 Polar Regions

THE OCEAN IN ITS MOST unlikely form can be found in the polar regions. Closest to the poles the ocean is constantly covered by a thick layer of ice around which the sea freezes over for at least part of the year. Biodiversity at these extreme latitudes is very low but some of the species living here are responsible for astonishing concentrations of biomass. During the short summer a seasonal abundance of nutrients is available. Sunshine almost around the clock fuels phytoplankton blooms in the polar seas. This abundant crop feeds the largest congregations of biomass on the planet, tiny crustaceans called krill. Krill is the keystone species in the Antarctic, and sustains the Southern Ocean food web. Mighty baleen whales, the largest creatures that ever lived on this planet, travel across the world's oceans all the way from the tropics to feed – their survival relies entirely on krill.

Both poles share a huge seasonal difference between summer and winter, far more intense than the tropical or even the temperate seas. While the summer Sun sets only for brief periods of time or even not at all, depending on the latitude, the opposite is true in winter. At the poles a day is six summer months long, the other six months is winter night. Somewhat surprisingly the poles receive the same amount of daylight per year as the equator, but the effects are quite different. At the poles the Sun is never overhead. Its warming radiation is largely absorbed on the long way through the atmosphere and the remainder is mostly reflected by the snow and ice cover. Of the Sun's heat, 85 percent is reflected back into space, in comparison to 5 percent in the open ocean. Because of their cold climate both polar regions have an important overall cooling effect on the rest of the planet.

But that is where the similarities end. Arctic and Antarctic lie literally, and metaphorically, poles apart. When it is summer at one pole, it is winter at the other. The Arctic is a frozen ocean almost completely surrounded by continents, whereas Antarctica is a frozen continent surrounded by a very cold ocean. Sea ice

under the sea ice or flee from the advancing winter. Thus the inhabitants of the Antarctic are either seasonal visitors, or permanent residents that have developed ways of dealing with the extreme cold. And Antarctica is cold – during winter it is the coldest place on Earth, with a record low temperature of -89°C measured in 1983. Antarctica is much colder than the Arctic due to its isolation from the rest of the world by strong westerly winds that circle the continent. This weather system supports the mighty circumpolar current – at 21,000 kilometres, the longest current in the world – that moves eastwards around the continent transporting a hundred times more water than all rivers in the world combined. Uninterrupted by any other land masses this current is so powerful it effectively blocks warmer ocean waters from mixing with the cold Antarctic ocean.

The seasonal feasting in Antarctica is based on huge amounts of phyto-plankton that grow in the upwellings of the nutrient rich Antarctic ocean during the summer months and lead to a population explosion of krill. If biomass is a measure of a species success, then krill must be considered one of the most successful species on the planet – with estimates of between 200 and 700 million tons of it growing every year. For comparison, the higher estimate represents over twice the total human biomass on the planet. Species of great baleen whales such as the humpbacks migrate into Antarctic waters during summer to gorge themselves on krill before they return to the tropics during winter for breeding. The krill supports an entire food web. In addition to the baleen whales, crab-eater seals, and penguins depend on krill as their main food source, and they in turn are harvested by the top predators of the Antarctic, the leopard seal and the killer whale.

Life in the ocean under the ice is surprisingly constant all year round. The water temperature stays fairly constant at -1.85°C, just above the temperature where seawater freezes, whatever the season. That makes it a fairly predictable home for the thriving invertebrate communities of this frigid environment.

regressing back to a juvenile state that needs less food. The few fish species that survive under the Antarctic sea ice employ chemicals in their blood that work like the antifreeze in a car radiator. Weddell seals are the only mammals that over-winter in the Antarctic, not counting humans. They rely on a thick layer of blubber but have to spend almost the entire winter under the ice in the relative warmth of the ocean water; coming up only for occasional gulps of extremely cold air in cracks and carefully maintained ice-free breathing holes.

Above the ice over-wintering is hardest. With freezing blizzards howling through the never-ending night only the toughest can survive these conditions that are worse than the average temperature on the surface of Mars. Emperor penguins are the only birds that over-winter in Antarctica, and surprisingly they do so in order to breed. This seemingly bizarre habit of breeding through the coldest winter night rather than moving to sunnier shores like other animals is explained once again by krill. Breeding through the winter gives the emperor penguin chicks a head start when the new krill season starts in spring. By then the chicks are ready to head for the water and spend the entire Antarctic summer building up a blubber layer that will protect them during the following winter.

One of the migrating species that leave Antarctica at the onset of winter are the Arctic terns, which stay in the Antarctic during the summer months and then migrate for their breeding season to the Arctic. At the end of the northern summer they return to the Antarctic for another summer, thus covering at least 40,000 kilometres per year.

Like the Arctic tern, many other Arctic species migrate with the seasons. Although the Arctic is quite mild in comparison with the Antarctic, temperatures still range between -50°C in winter and +10°C in summer. For most animals that temperature difference is reason enough to leave during the coldest months. However under its thick ice cover the Arctic Ocean also stays at a reasonably

constant temperature just above freezing all year round, which has a stabilizing effect on the climate, keeping the summers cool but the winters relatively warm – compared with the Antarctic that is. Productivity in the Arctic is patchy and seasonal. Many large rivers drain their relatively warm freshwater and a huge sediment load into the Arctic Ocean, leading to brackish surface waters and short but explosive phytoplankton blooms along the fringes of the sea ice during spring.

In contrast to the Antarctic the sea ice of the Arctic is ruled by land predators, in particular the polar bear. While wolves venture only a short distance from shore out on to the sea ice and snow foxes often live in the shadow of hunting polar bears, hoping for scraps, it is the polar bear that is best adapted to the live on, and between, the ice floes. Polar bears are so well-attuned to life in the Arctic Ocean that they are considered marine mammals. They have been sighted swimming in open waters, 90 kilometres away from the nearest shore. During winter polar bears roam widely across the frozen sea ice and hunt for seals along their breathing holes. In spring and summer they swim between ice floes where seals give birth to their pups and feed them. The seals have adjusted to the hunting pressure, by reducing their nursing period to just a few days in which they are highly vulnerable. Hooded seals nurse only for four days, the shortest lactation period of any mammal. The pup is fed with milk that contains over 60 percent fat and doubles its weight in just those few days before it is abandoned by its mother who directly mates again with a male that has been guarding her from other suitors by hanging out on a neighbouring ice floe.

This chapter concludes our exploration of the shallow fringes, which include the most diverse and colourful ocean habitats. In the next section we will dare the journey out into the vast and seemingly limitless space of the open ocean where life has to come to terms with quite a different set of challenges.

Sooty albatross

— 0 m

┌
│
└
— 2 m

Phoebetria palpebrata
Size: 2 metres

The soaring light-mantled sooty albatross in the centre of the picture has a wingspan of more than two metres. That gives an impression of the scale of the surf at the exposed western coastline of the Auckland Islands. Located in the 'Furious Fifties', these subantarctic islands are battered by strong westerly winds that circle the globe.

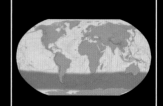

Sooty shearwater

0 m

– 70 m

Puffinus griseus
Size: 95 centimetres

A sooty shearwater 'flies' underwater on the hunt for fish. Shearwaters are truly at home in both elements. Masters of the air, they migrate on the wing halfway around the world, travelling up to 70,000 kilometres a year and are capable of covering over 500 kilometres per day. Underwater, they have been observed to dive to a depth of almost 70 metres in search of food.

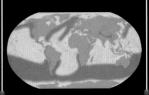

Snares crested penguins

0 m

Eudyptes robustus
Size: 55 centimetres

Like torpedoes, Snares crested penguins launch themselves into the sea at high speed and under a fringe of bull kelp on the subantarctic Snares Islands. Penguins are often nervous at the shoreline and prefer to seek safety in numbers before they dare a speedy plunge into the ocean, where a predator may be lying

Southern right whale

┌ 0 m

Eubalaena australis

Size: 17 metres

An inquisitive southern right whale calf passes within touching distance of the photographer. Once considered the 'right whale' for slaughter by whalers because they are relatively slow and do not sink when harpooned, these gentle giants are slowly recovering from the brink of extinction thanks to the whale sanctuary in

Ice floes

0 m

Around the entire continent of Antarctica the ocean is covered with sea ice as far as the eye can see. During the summer months it breaks up into ice floes, allowing air-breathing animals from whales to penguins access to the incredible bounty beneath – krill. The entire food-web in the Antarctic is based on this one

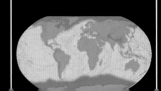

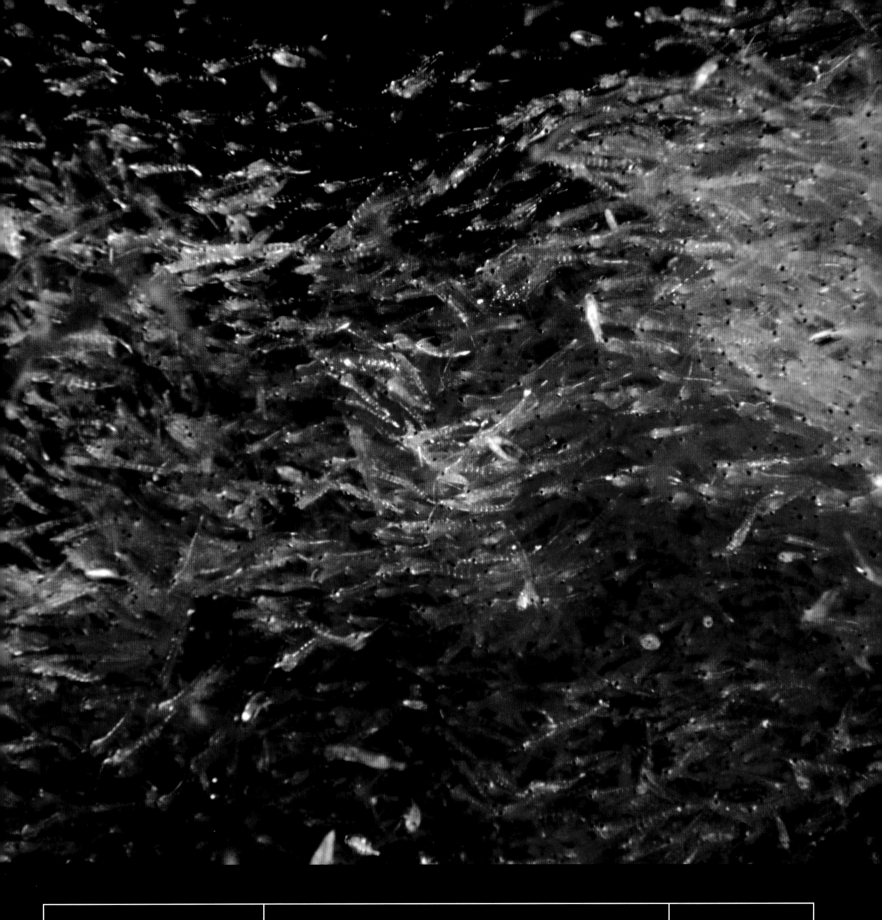

Krill

0 m

200 m

Family Euphausiidae
Size: 6 centimetres

Feeding on seasonal blooms of phytoplankton and zooplankton the krill population explodes during the summer months, feeding in turn the largest animals on the planet, the baleen whales. In an attempt to avoid their predators most krill species, like this Pacific krill, make a daily vertical migration – swimming down into the twilight zone during the daylight hours and returning to the surface at night to feed.

Antarctic pursuit I

0 m
200 m

Seal: Hydrurga leptonyx
Penguin: Pygoscelis papua
Size: 3 metres / 0.9 metres

A leopard seal and a Gentoo penguin are facing off. Both are extremely swift swimmers, perfectly adapted to the watery element with sleek and torpedo-shaped bodies. But the penguin is swimming for its life, trying to outmanoeuvre the dangerous predator by feigning and suddenly changing direction like a hare hunted by a fox.

Antarctic pursuit II

— 0 m

— 200 m

Seal: Hydrurga leptonyx
Penguin: Pygoscelis papua
Size: 3 metres / 0.9 metres

The leopard seal is rapidly closing in, tiring the penguin by its constant chasing. Leopard seals are formidable hunters and penguins are among the favourite prey of adult seals. But surprisingly about half of their diet is made up of tiny krill — the sharp teeth of the seal have serrated edges that can be used to sieve off water when catching krill.

Antarctic pursuit III

0 m
200 m

Seal: Hydrurga leptonyx
Penguin: Pygoscelis papua
Size: 3 metres / 0.9 metres

With the exhausted penguin in its jaws the leopard seal comes up for a breath of air. It will stay at the surface to thrash the penguin around until the carcass breaks up into bite-sized chunks. Leopard seals rank next to the killer whale (orca) as top predators in the Antarctic and will attack humans. Killer whales are their only natural enemy.

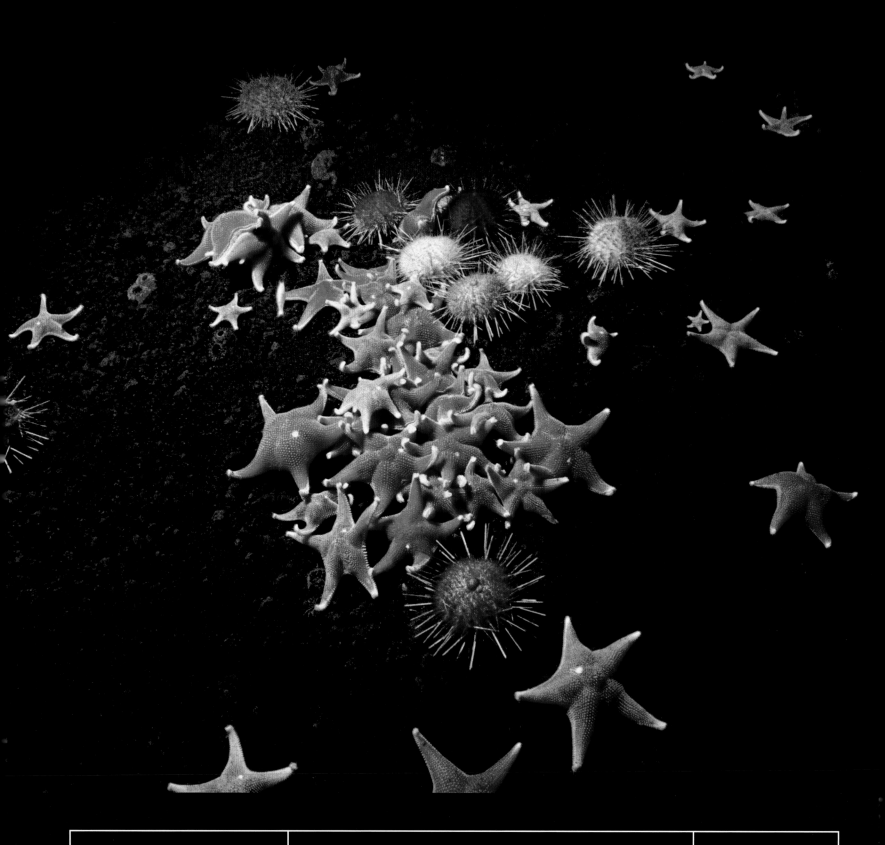

Red starfish

0 m	
>30 m	

Odontaster validus
Size: 7 centimetres

Forming a dense cluster among a group of sea urchins the red starfish is the most abundant starfish around the Antarctic coastline. Experiments have shown they can chemically sense whether other starfish in the vicinity are starved or well fed and are strongly attracted to those that have had a good feed. This sort of gatecrashing is a perfect homing device to find rich but patchy food sources.

Weddell seal

0 m	Leptonychotes weddellii
	Size: 3 metres
700 m	

Famous for their ability to dive as deep as 700 metres and to hold their breath for extended periods of up to 80 minutes, Weddell seals also hold another record. They are the southernmost naturally occurring mammal in the world. Only humans venture further south. They are also one of the very few hardy species that over-winter in the Antarctic.

Nemertina worms

0 m

—>30 m

Parborlasia corrugatus
Size: 1.5 metres

Over one metre long, nemertina worms congregate to feed on a jellyfish. Being ferocious omnivores these worms eat almost anything in their path. Nemertinas lack a respiratory system and move slowly, taking in oxygen through their skin from the surrounding water. They can regulate their oxygen intake by stretching and flattening their bodies to increase their surface area when needed.

Sea angel

0 m		Clione limacina
		Size: 5 centimetres
200 m		

This angelic apparition hovering on wing-like flaps amongst the plankton in the Southern Ocean is really a ferocious predatory snail. Preying on its shelled cousins, it grabs them in the blink of an eye with specialized tentacles and hooks – like a boarding party from a pirate ship. The actual ingestion of its quarry is a much slower process that may take an hour or longer.

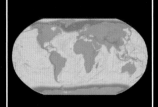

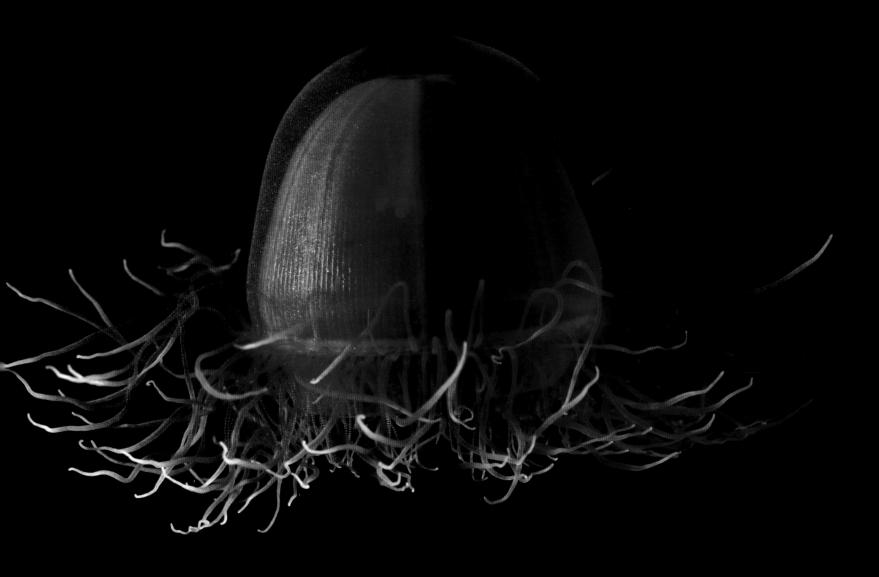

Arctic jellyfish

200 m

4000 m

Crossota norvegica
Size: 2 centimetres

Composed of more than 95 percent water, hydromedusas are among the most fragile marine animals, and also represent one of the oldest, most primitive groups in the animal kingdom. However, behind their ephemeral beauty these simple creatures are very capable predators that catch and stun zooplankton and small fish with their trailing tentacles.

Greenland shark

0 m

Somniosus microcephalus
Size: 6 metres

At more than six metres in length the Greenland Shark is one of the largest sharks in the world and the biggest fish in the Arctic. These sharks are often referred to as 'sleeper sharks' because of their sluggish movements – but that perception may be misplaced, as parts of a horse and even an entire

Walrus

0 m

—200 m

Odobenus rosmarus
Size: 3.5 metres

This herd of female walruses is migrating in the Arctic pack ice with a calf.
Walruses are very gregarious, forming herds that may have thousands of members.
However the sexes live quite separate lives outside the mating season with a well
established social structure within each herd. Both sexes bear tusks used solely
for social displays. They play an important role in maintaining the 'pecking' order.

Polar bear

0 m

5 m

Ursus maritimus
Size: 3 metres

Polar bears, the top predators in the Arctic, are such good swimmers that they are officially considered marine mammals. They have been encountered swimming in open water up to 90 kilometres off the coast. The recent retreat of Arctic pack ice is forcing polar bears to swim unusually long distances in the summer — and several drownings have been reported.

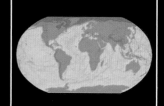

Harp seal

Phoca groenlandica

Size: 2.2 metres

A harp seal surfacing at a breathing hole in the Arctic pack-ice. Harp seals live most of the year entirely within the boundaries of the ice. They migrate up to 2,500 kilometres with the retreating ice to their summer feeding grounds and then return to the south in autumn as the ocean refreezes.

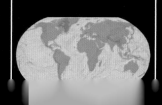

ON THE HIGH SEAS

LEFT *Under foreboding skies a Southern Ocean storm reaches full fury. Lashed by winds of over 100 kilometres per hour for days at a time, waves can grow higher than a three-storey building. Extreme weather plays a vital role in the ocean ecosystem, mixing vital nutrients into the sunlit upper layer. In cooler seas, winter gales are predictably followed by plankton blooms in spring.*

5 Open Ocean

FAR AWAY FROM THE MURKY COASTAL SEAS lies the unforgettable blue of the open ocean. A world without walls, its scale is overwhelming – 100 million square miles of interconnected space. Only here could a whale the size of an airliner seem dwarfed by the vastness of its surroundings, or a jellyfish live out its life without ever encountering a hard surface. This is the pelagic realm, home to animals adapted to a life suspended or swimming in open space. Snorkelling at the surface, human interlopers often find themselves feeling uncomfortably exposed, looking down at the dancing veils of sunlight pointing to the dark abyss, far below.

Beyond the wide, shallow shelves fringing the continents the sea floor drops away rapidly to ocean basins with an average depth of more than two miles. Out here, even in the clearest tropical seawater, sunlight struggles to penetrate more than a few hundred metres with any strength. Marine plants – mostly microscopic phytoplankton – cannot live any deeper. Like all plants, they need sunlight to grow; and so the ocean's invisible meadows are restricted to a thin upper layer, a mere one percent of total ocean depth. This is the photic zone, the vital skin of the oceanic apple, and the solar energy captured by phytoplankton powers almost the entire ocean ecosystem, from the surface down to the abyssal sea floor.

In the sunlit zone tiny herbivorous browsers harvest the many kinds of phytoplankton, scooping up glassy diatoms and chasing down fast-swimming green dinoflagellates (in the open ocean even vegetarians need to catch their dinner). These browsers, chiefly tiny crustaceans, are in turn hunted by predators, which are eaten by larger predators, and so on. Among the most important oceanic predators are the jellies, the stinging medusae and the beautiful comb jellies, which shimmer with iridescence and snare prey with sticky tentacles. These are joined by other mid-level predators, small fishes and squid, and the top hunters: tunas, marlins, sharks, dolphins and whales.

Among the most specialized inhabitants of the sunlit layer are the 'blue fleet' – a menagerie of invertebrates that live only at the very surface of the ocean, often buoyed up by floats. With few exceptions these animals have blue or violet hues, an effective camouflage. The most famous of these is the vibrant but formidable Portuguese man-of-war jellyfish, whose long trailing tentacles have caused misery for many a bather. They are kept afloat by a gas bladder filled with carbon monoxide, a gas found in car exhaust fumes. The float doubles as a sail, so these jellies are susceptible to the vagaries of the wind, often washing ashore in their millions during stormy weather. Goose barnacles also sail the seas, attached to floating driftwood or, increasingly, plastic and glass rubbish. One species secretes its own float of rubbery white foam; so equipped, they travel great distances, catching plankton with a basket of feeding appendages.

Sargassum seaweed, the only floating seaweed, occurs in the Sargasso Sea and travels into the North Atlantic via the Gulf Stream current. Its dense branches are a refuge to a diverse community of invertebrates and a variety of fish, including the superbly camouflaged Sargussum anglerfish, a close relative of the deep-water anglers found in the black water below. In the temperate zones, kelp plants often detach from the sea floor and drift out to sea. These rafts act as a magnet for animals that crave the security of cover, or perhaps simply a break in the monotony of their blue surroundings. These include ocean sunfish, some weighing a tonne, which often congregate around floating kelp.

One way or another, deep-sea creatures living in the darkness below the surface zone must get a share of the sun's bounty to survive. Food scraps make their way into deep waters in many forms, ranging from sinking clumps of dead phytoplankton to faecal pellets expelled by jellies. Undoubtedly the ultimate windfall for deep-water scavengers are the giant carcasses of dead whales, whose arrival on the abyssal sea floor spawns a feast that can last for years. Many deep-water species don't leave things to chance and take purposeful nightly trips up to the productive surface layer to feed in this relatively food-rich environment, arriving under cover of darkness. Upon their return to the depths, these commuters are picked off one by one by toothy predators skulking in the darkness – unwittingly transporting energy from the upper layers down to the deep-sea ecosystem in the process.

In contrast to the deeper layers the open ocean offers rich pickings, yet it is an underwater desert, compared to the coastal seas. Its intense blue colour is a clear sign that phytoplankton are few, although on occasion dense blooms of phytoplankton turn the seawater a soupy green. Invariably this event is closely followed by a population explosion of grazing animals such as copepod crustaceans, multitudinous, one-eyed 'insects of the sea'. Salps, tubular jelly-like creatures, also go into reproductive overdrive when the phytoplankton bloom, budding off their offspring like bullets from a machine gun. Each individual produces an intricate net made from mucus in its gill cavity, with which it snares microscopically small particles with clinical efficiency. Fast-growing and numerous, a salp swarm soon denudes the water column of phytoplankton, whereupon they all die and sink.

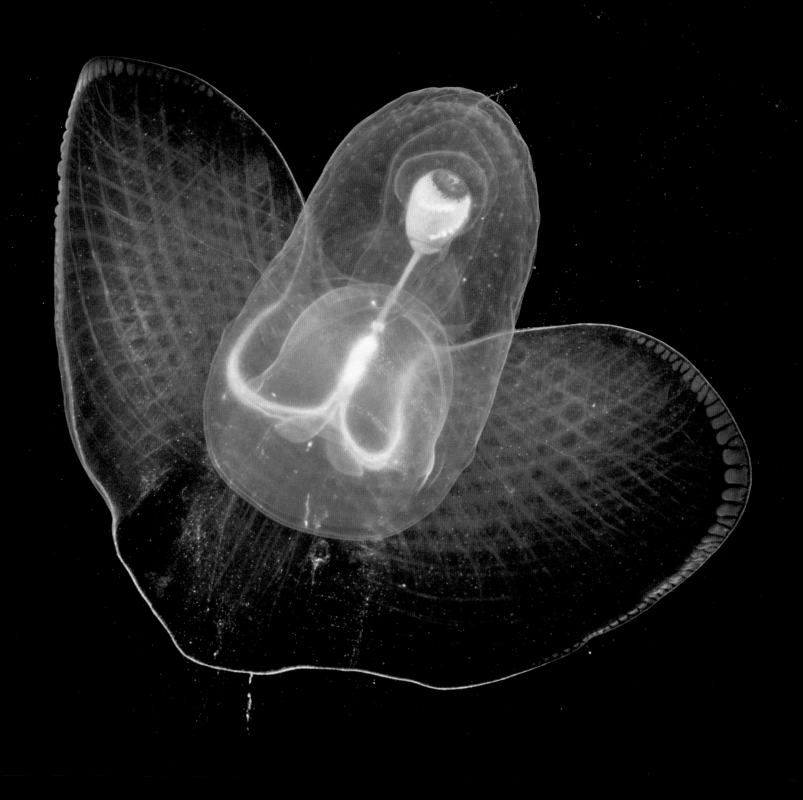

Sea butterfly

0 m

1000 m

Corolla calceola
Size: 4 centimetres

In defiance of its snail ancestry, the sea butterfly flaps its wings to 'fly' beneath the ocean. A specialized feeder, this hand-sized animal secretes a sticky bed-sheet sized web of mucus – a drift net for the smallest plankton. So equipped, it sinks slowly through the water column before reeling in its trap and consuming the innumerable tiny organisms and organic particles it has snared.

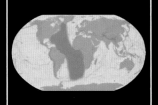

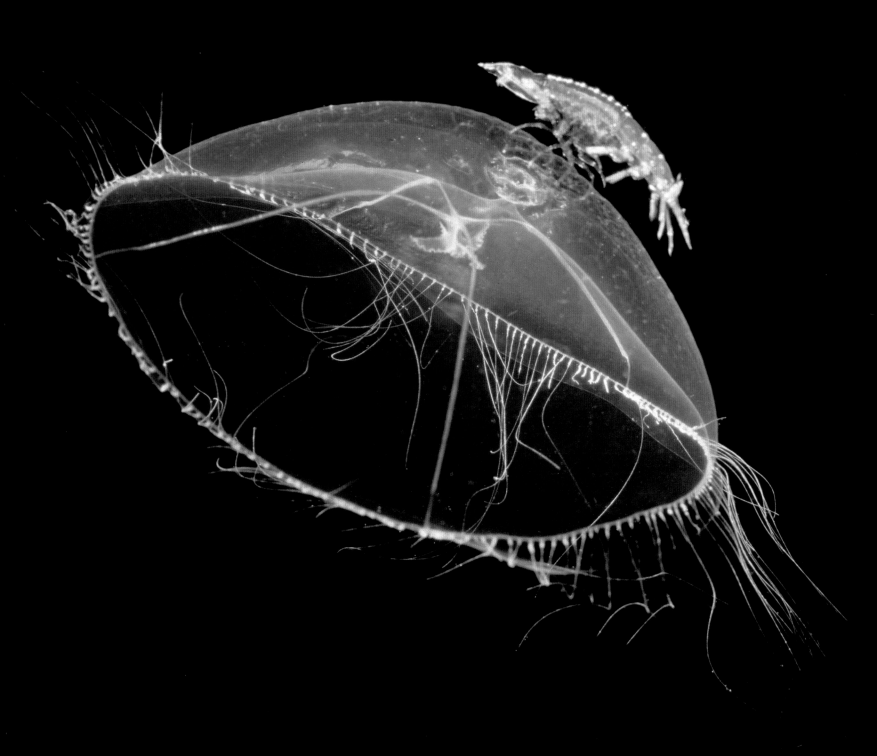

Cross jellyfish & amphipod

0 m

200 m

Mitrocoma cellularia
Size: 10 centimetres

An amphipod crustacean perches atop the bell of a cross jelly, riding it through the ocean. Although it has long been known that these two animal groups – jellies and amphipods – frequently live together, the reasons are not well understood. In most cases it seems the amphipod feeds on the jelly, somehow avoiding being stung by the stinging tentacles.

Blue button

0 m

−1 m

Porpita porpita
Size: 1 centimetre

This little blue button, or porpita, is about a centimetre across. Each jelly is actually a colony composed of many different individuals, each modified to form a particular part of the whole animal. Part of the diverse 'blue fleet' that floats at the ocean surface, it catches microscopic plankton. These ocean wanderers wash ashore in their millions following stormy weather.

Portuguese man-of-war

0 m
1 m

Physalia physalis
Size: 1 metre

The Portuguese man-of-war has a float and a sail, and so equipped can travel large distances, trailing a net of feeding tentacles behind it. Despite a reputation as a vicious stinger, at home on the high seas it rarely encounters swimmers. It is when they are blown, en masse, into shallow coastal bays that they become a problem, making some beaches seasonally unswimmable.

151

Salp chain

⌐0 m

─1000 m

Pegea sp.
Size: 60 centimetres

Like a gelatinous ammunition belt, a chain of salps makes an incongruous sight.
Each 'unit' is a separate individual capable of surviving independently. More
closely related to humans than to the jellyfish they resemble, salps reproduce
and grow with remarkable rapidity. In the right conditions they can form vast
swarms, all but stripping the ocean of phytoplankton as they browse.

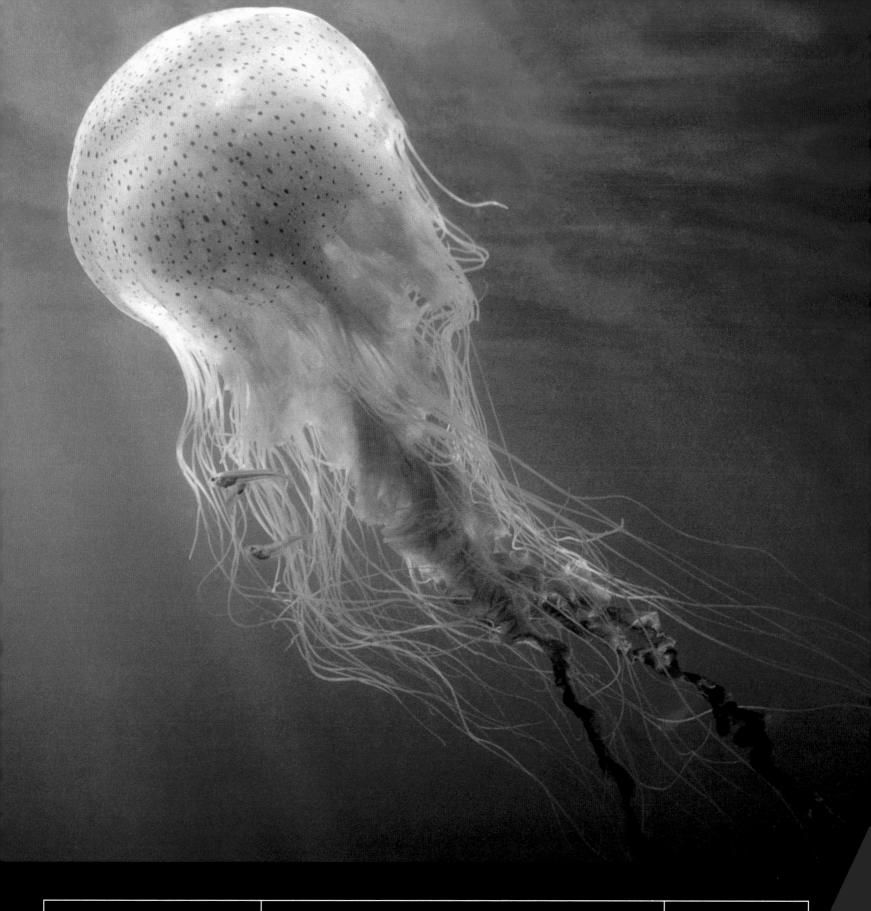

Sea nettle

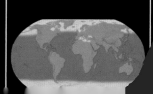

0 m

Chrysaora sp

Size: 30 centimetres

A large jellyfish pulsates slowly through oceanic waters. The physical support of this watery medium has enabled the evolution of body plans that simply could not work on land; there is a good reason there are no land jellies. This is why the ocean has 28 animal phyla – the broadest divisions of animal life – whereas

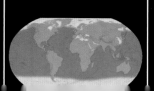

Buoy barnacles

0 m

Dosima fascicularis
Size: 5 centimetres

One group of marine animals not known for globetrotting is the barnacles.
However, the buoy barnacle builds itself a spongy float and embarks on a life
spent bobbing along at the ocean surface. These relatives of shrimps and crabs
have legs modified for sieving plankton from the water, and a protective casing

Sargassum anglerfish

⌐0 m

Histrio histrio

Size: 15 centimetres

The Sargasso Sea, off the eastern United States, is famous for its floating mats of Sargassum, the only seaweed adapted for life on the open ocean. Among this alga's most cryptic residents is the superbly camouflaged anglerfish — *Histrio histrio* — which literally means 'actor'. It lures prey with its forehead-mounted

Chambered nautilus

0 m

Nautilus pompilius

Size: 25 centimetres

Nautiluses are 'living fossils' – sole survivors of a once-important group of animals that flourished in the oceans half a billion years ago. These alienesque deep-water cephalopods produce the much prized shells, but the creatures themselves are rarely seen. Unlike octopuses, which have but eight arms,

Chambered nautilus

0 m

Nautilus pompilius
Size: 25 centimetres

Up close, a nautilus head is a mass of tentacles at the base of which lies an odd, expressionless eye. Largely unchanged for hundreds of millions of years this eye works on the same principle as a pinhole camera and forms a blurry but serviceable image. Like a snail, the nautilus can retract into its spiral shell

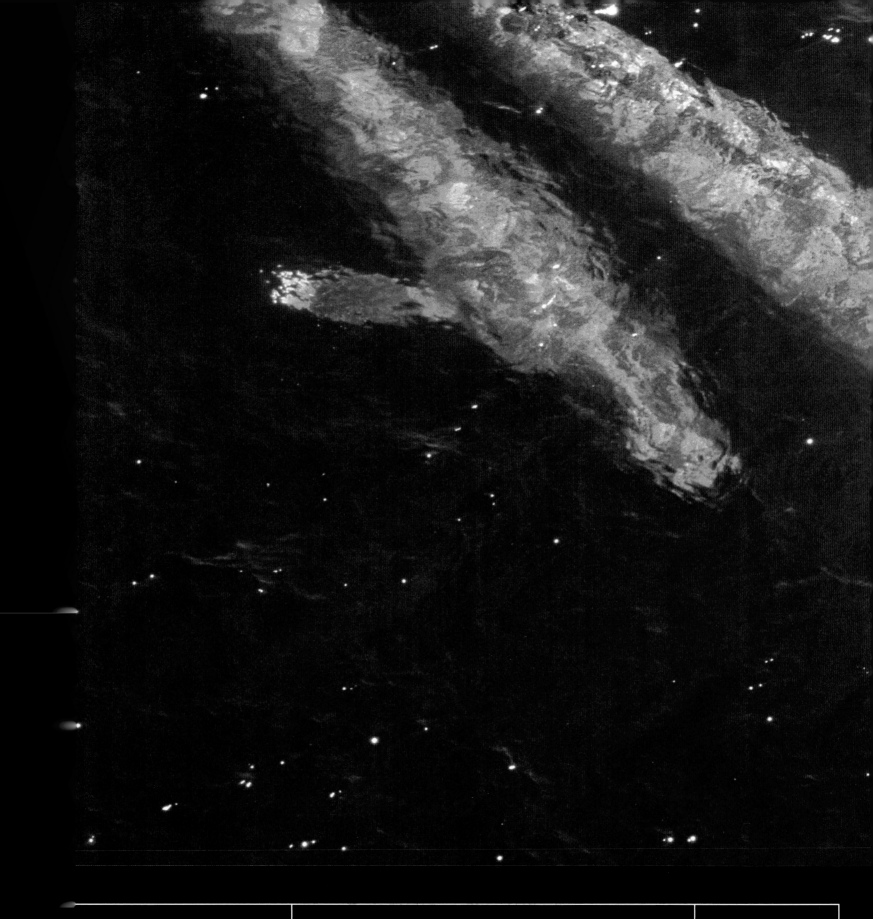

Blue whales

0 m

Balaenoptera musculus

Size: 33 metres

A blue whale mother and calf swim in the ocean off California. The great whales' ability to catch tiny plankton prey gives these leviathans access to a plentiful food source, enabling them to reach great sizes: indeed, this species is thought to be the largest animal that has ever lived, growing up to 33.5 metres long – only

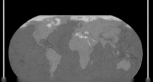

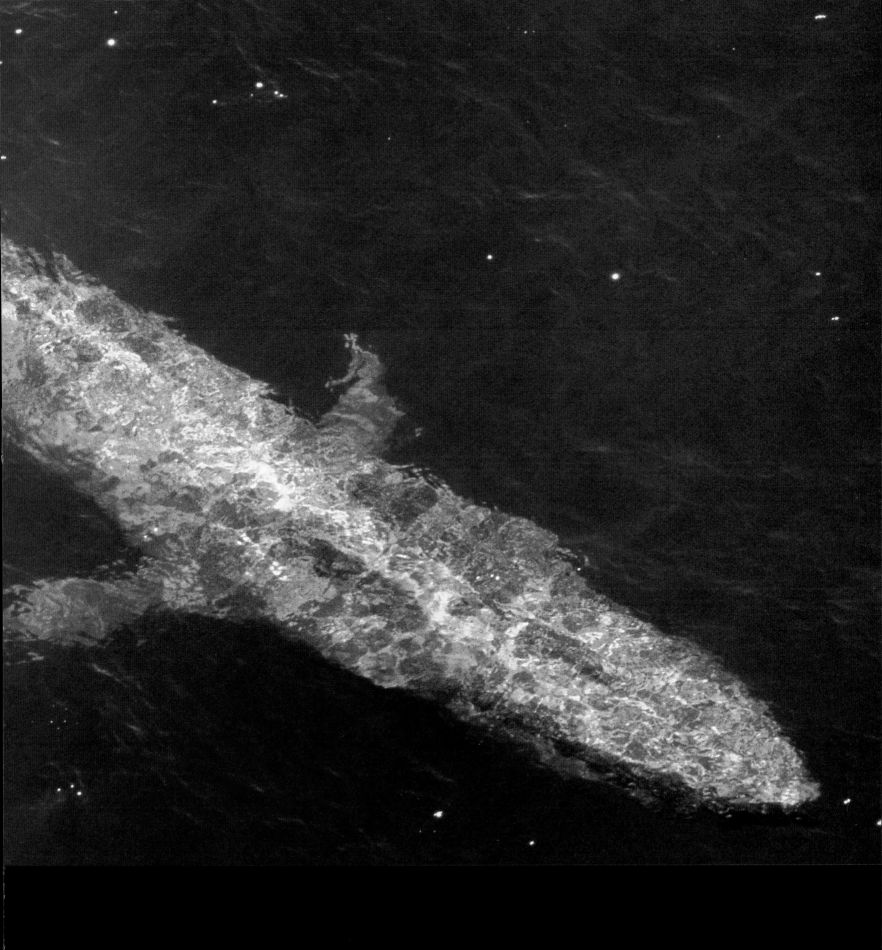

Whale shark

0 m

−1000 m

Rhincodon typus
Size: 12 metres

A shark as big as a whale? The whale shark is by far the world's largest living fish, growing up to 12 metres long. Like many of the largest animals in the ocean, they are harmless plankton feeders. The whale shark's habit of turning up in the same place year after year has made them an important tourist attraction in the Indo-Pacific.

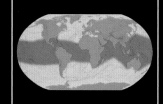

Common dolphins

Delphinus delphis
Size: 2 metres

− 1000 m

A pod of common dolphins tracks purposefully across the ocean. Thought to be the world's commonest cetacean, their pods can contain thousands of individuals. They are often seen over the continental shelf, but are also at home in the open ocean. Enthusiastic hunters of fish and squid, they are an acrobatic and vocal species, and, being highly gregarious, they seldom go unnoticed.

Great white shark

0 m

— 1000 m

Carcharodon carcharias
Size: 5 metres

Thanks to the movie *Jaws*, the great white shark is one the most feared and misunderstood animals in the sea. But attitudes are changing. Several nations, including South Africa and New Zealand, have banned the capture and killing of these majestic sharks. Once regarded as coast-dwellers, satellite tagging has recently revealed that great whites set off on long migrations across the ocean.

Ocean sunfish

0 m
−1000 m

Mola mola
Size: 3 metres

The ocean sunfish *Mola mola* (the scientific name means 'millstone') is among the largest of all bony fishes, weighing up to a tonne. They scull gracefully through the open ocean, picking up surprising speed once they have gained momentum. Sunfish have small mouths, containing bony plates composed of fused teeth and feed mainly on jellyfishes, salps and other gelatinous zooplankton.

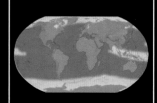

Blue shark

┌ 0 m
│
└ — 350 m

Prionace glauca
Size: 3.8 metres

Dappled with sunlight, a blue shark swims effortlessly through the upper ocean. One of the commonest sharks in the world, they are migratory wanderers; a typical individual will travel tens of thousands of kilometres in its lifetime. Blue sharks enjoy a broad diet of fish and squid augmented by occasional scavenging.

ROV

0 m

3000 m

Size: 2 metres

A remotely operated vehicle (ROV) is deployed from its mothership to explore the depths. Attached by a tether, it is controlled by a pilot aboard the ship. Video cameras and powerful lights are the ROV's eyes, while a mechanical claw functions as its hands. Robotic vehicles like these are gradually replacing manned submersibles as the primary means of exploring deep-sea habitats.

6 The Deep

IT IS OFTEN SAID WE LIVE ON A BLUE PLANET, but perhaps 'black planet' is a more fitting description. More than nine tenths of Earth's inhabitable volume is cloaked in perpetual darkness, far beyond the reach of even the dimmest sunlight. This is the deep ocean, the world's largest and least-known ecosystem, with an average depth of almost four kilometres. Here unseen and undiscovered creatures live out their lives in total anonymity. In an age when far-flung and remote lands have been transformed into little more than exotic holiday destinations, 'The Deep' retains its mystery and frontier status.

Early oceanographers thought that beyond a certain depth the ocean must be lifeless. It stood to good reason: the abyss was known to be a realm of eternal darkness, cold, and relentless pressure. How could anything survive in such an impossible place? This 'azoic theory', as it came to be known, was widely accepted by early Victorian naturalists. But a series of pioneering expeditions, most notably the epic voyage of the Royal Navy's *Challenger*, proved that life could in fact live at great depths. In 1872 the once-formidable warship began a four-year global exploration that laid down the foundations of modern oceanography in spectacular fashion (it took 50 hefty volumes to just describe its findings). Everywhere that *Challenger*'s nets and dredges were deployed yielded life. Nearly a century later the bathyscaphe *Trieste*, an ultra-deep diving submarine, descended to the bottom of the Marianas Trench, the deepest place on Earth. There, nearly 11 kilometres below the waves, *Trieste*'s pilot Jacques Piccard witnessed a flatfish and a shrimp, and the azoic theory was finally extinguished.

To descend in a submersible to the deep-sea floor entails a journey through three zones, each one populated by a distinctive community of animals. The sunlit layer of the open ocean is only 100 to 200 metres thick and soon gives way to the mesopelagic realm, where dim twilight conditions prevail. Although light levels are low, predators with well-adapted eyes abound, and an elaborate game of cat-and-mouse ensues. A vital tactic is disguise, and most mesopelagic animals are transparent or a highly reflective silver to blend into this shadowy world. In the deeper reaches of the mesopelagic zone, many fishes, squid and shrimps are orange or red, a seemingly odd colour choice; in fact, at depth these colours appear black or dark brown due to the absorption of red light in seawater. Well equipped for low-light situations, many twilight zone animals swim towards the surface to feed each night, returning home just before dawn, collectively the largest mass migration on Earth.

The giant squid *Architeuthis dux* is perhaps the most famous inhabitant of the mesopelagic zone. Immortalized by Disney's film adaptation of Jules Verne's *20,000 Leagues Under the Sea*, they grow to at least 12 metres long and 300 kilograms in weight. Despite their bulk, the squid's preferred prey are squid, fishes and shrimps a tiny fraction of their size. In 2007, the giant squid lost its status as the largest known invertebrate when a 'colossal squid', *Mesonychoteuthis hamiltoni* weighing half a tonne was captured in the cold waters off Antarctica. *Mesonychoteuthis* is a far more fearsome animal than the giant squid. With stout muscular body and its arms and tentacles equipped with large talon-like hooks, it hunts large prey, like the man-sized Patagonian toothfish.

Below the mesopelagic lies the bathypelagic zone. Here darkness is total except for the ghostly blue-green glow of bioluminescence. The entrancing ability of some organisms to make their own light is the norm in the deep sea – it is estimated that 80 percent of deep-sea animals can glow, and this ability has evolved independently in almost all major animal groups, ranging from worms to sharks. The light itself is produced by a fairly simple chemical reaction; some deep-sea animals produce it themselves, while others subcontract the task to symbiotic bacteria. Clearly bioluminescence fulfils a useful role in the daily lives of the deep-sea dwellers, and finding out exactly what that role may be for different species is a fascinating field of research. Anglerfishes, for example, use the glowing tips of their head-mounted 'fishing rods' to lure prey, while many mesopelagic fishes – the hatchetfishes, dragonfishes and bristlemouths – have glowing bellies to disguise their silhouettes from below. Some squids, shrimps and fishes can squirt out glowing mucus to confuse predators, and possibly attract the predator's predators. Some jellies flash brightly in an intimidating display of light. Male and female lanternfishes have different patterns of lights on their bodies, so perhaps this helps them to distinguish their mates in the darkness.

Surviving in the abyss is a challenge, but not an insurmountable one. The immense water pressure has little negative effect on deep-sea animals, whose bodies exist at the same pressure as their surroundings – much as our own bodies are acclimatized to atmospheric pressure. Perpetual darkness, too, is not in itself lethal, but it does prevent plants from growing, so the deep-sea food supply is rather sparse. It is mostly limited to the rain of organic matter sinking from the sunlit zone. Finding the next meal is the greatest challenge facing deep-water life. This is why most abyssal creatures swim or crawl in what seems to us to be slow motion, thereby conserving as much energy as possible. Likewise,

RIGHT *Daggers of ice, the glinting teeth of the lancetfish,* Alepisaurus brevirostris, *are a menacing presence in the deep. Growing to two metres in length, these barracuda-like fish are high-speed predators that hunt a wide variety of prey, even juvenile giant squid.*

they need to grasp all meal opportunities with vigour, and nowhere is this more obvious than on the mud-covered plains of the deep-sea floor. Down here, scavengers such as hagfish, brittlestars and amphipod crustaceans arrive in droves to feast on sunken carcasses, stripping them to bones in a matter of hours. Smaller organic particles like clumps of dead phytoplankton are mopped up by armies of sea cucumbers, which march across the deep plains en masse in search of food. These unassuming creatures can make up to nine-tenths of the seafloor biomass and so are among Earth's dominant lifeforms.

The deep sea has yielded some quite astonishing secrets as new methods of ocean exploration have developed. The discovery of the first hydrothermal vents by the manned submersible *Alvin* in the mid-1970s rocked the oceanography world. These undersea hot springs are dotted along the world's mid-ocean ridges, where incomprehensible tectonic forces lead to sea floor spreading and the creation of new sea floor. Here, black smokers can be found, gothic chimneys composed of minerals precipitated from super-heated fluids gushing from fissures in the oceanic crust. At temperatures reaching 400°C, the chimneys' mineral-laden 'smoke' is hot enough to melt lead (and the viewports of careless submarines).

In the food-deprived deep, hydrothermal vents are veritable oases of life, with a food chain based on bacteria nourished by the toxic chemicals spewing from the active smokers. So the vent-dwellers rely on the Earth's internal energy, and not the sun, to power their lives – a mode of life called chemosynthesis. Most spectacular of them all is the giant tubeworm *Riftia pachyptila*, which grows to more than two metres long. Its leathery white tube and scarlet feeding plumes are an iconic sight in the pages of *National Geographic* and it is sobering to think that they were unknown a few decades ago. Along with giant clams, mussels and many hundreds of other species, giant tubeworms are part of a lush and strange ecosystem that is as close to life on another planet as it is possible to find on Earth. One can only wonder what other undiscovered marvels lie hidden from sight in the dark depths of the global ocean.

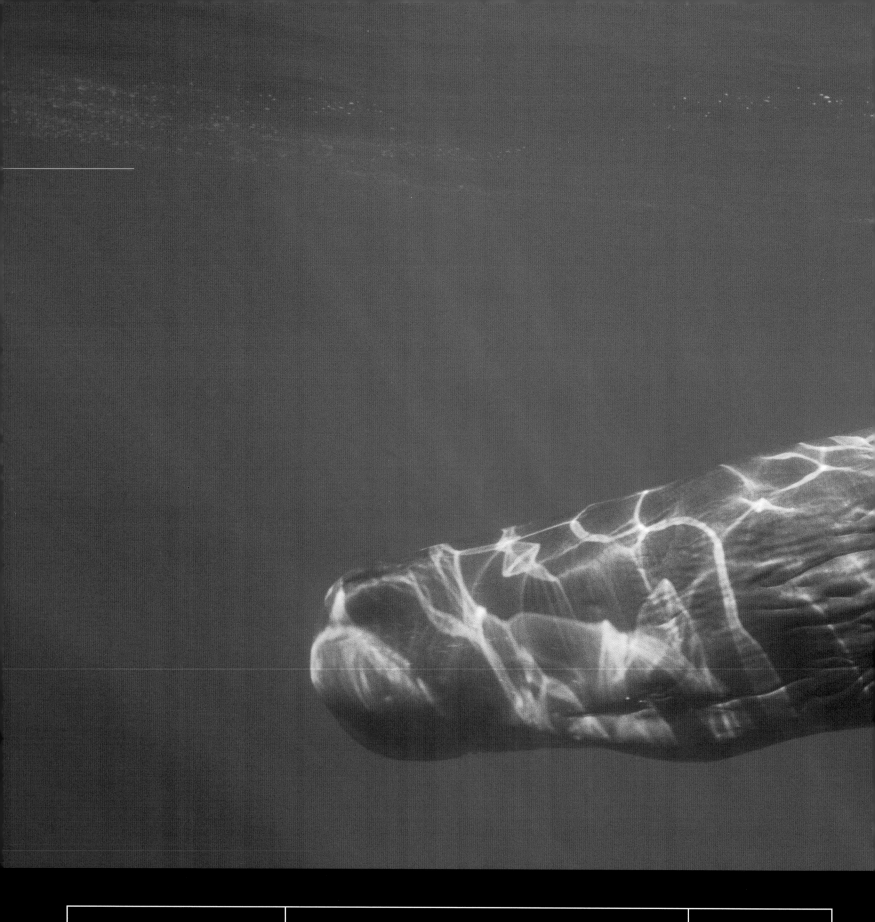

Sperm whale

0 m

Physeter macrocephalus
Size: 20 metres

1500 m

A sperm whale prepares for a dive into the deep ocean, where it hunts chiefly for squid, including, most famously, the giant squid. In fact such epic encounters are relatively rare – even a 40-tonne bull sperm whale feeds mostly on small squid. Foraging dives as deep as 1,500 metres and lasting 80 minutes have been recorded.

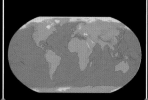

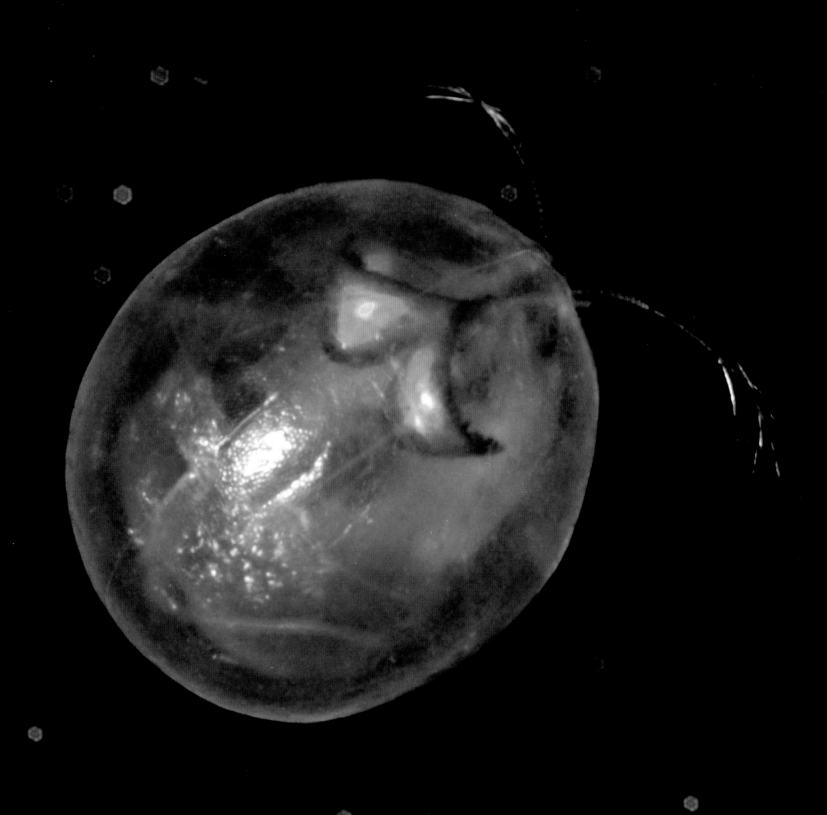

Giant ostracod

200 m

Gigantocypris muelleri
1.5 centimetres

1000 m

The giant ostracod *Gigantocypris* is a strange and rarely seen inhabitant of the twilight zone. Its orange marble-sized body is propelled haphazardly by a pair of antennae that reveal the animal's crustacean heritage. The giant ostracod's large and reflective eyes aid this unlikely predator in surprising nimbler prey such as small fishes and arrow worms.

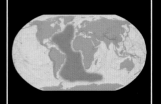

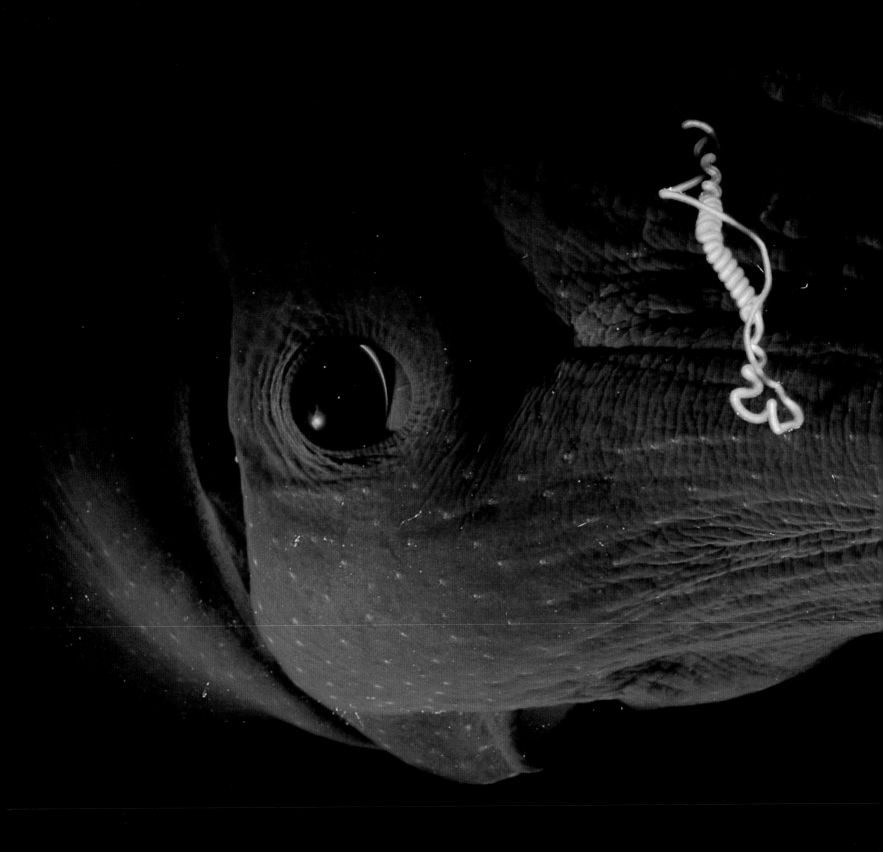

Vampire squid

Vampyroteuthis infernalis

Size: 30 centimetres

With an undeserved Latin name that literally means 'vampire squid from hell', this animal has a curious mix of squid and octopus features. Living in the dark, oxygen-poor layer of the deep ocean, the vampire squid is completely covered in light organs and can emit glowing mucus when threatened, a decoy to predators. It preys mainly upon deepwater jellies and crustaceans.

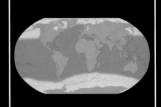

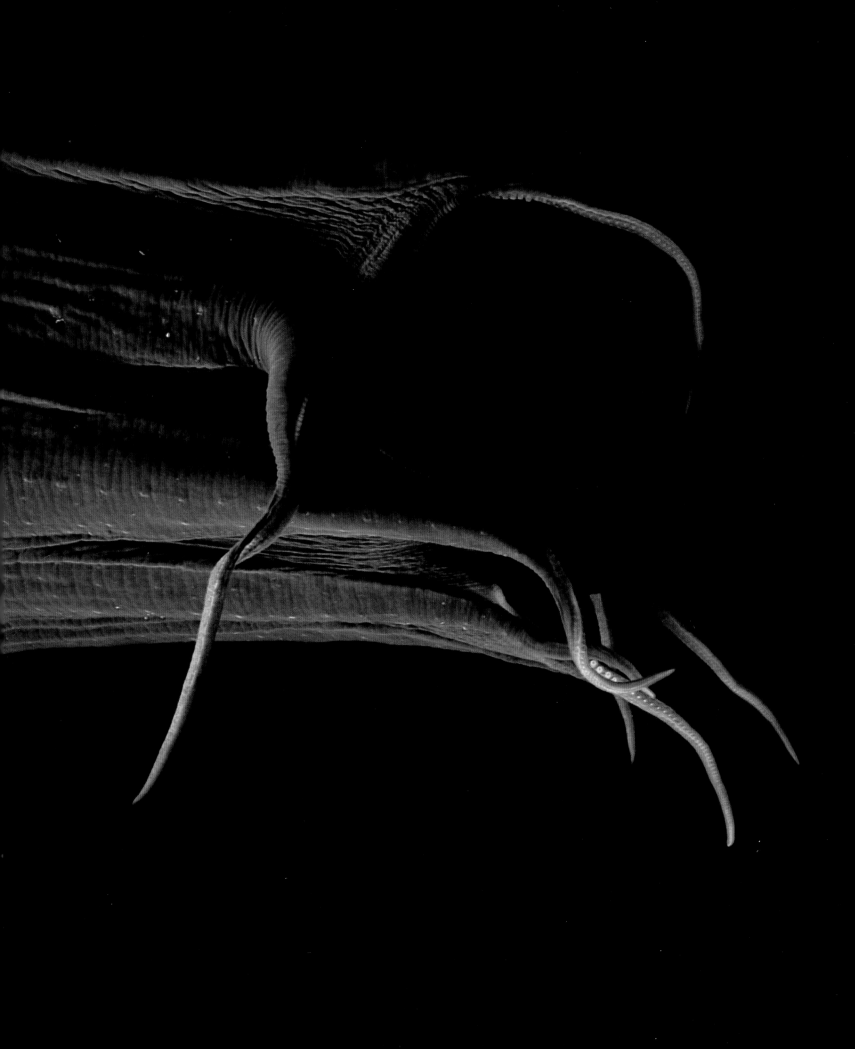

Scaly dragonfish

200 m
1500 m

Stomias boa boa
Size: 30 centimetres

With sharp teeth, bioluminescent lure and myriad light organs running along its body, the scaly dragonfish is a classic mid-water fish. Occurring at depths from 200 to 1,500 metres in tropical to subpolar climes, it preys on small fishes and planktonic crustaceans, and commonly migrates to shallower depths to feed each night.

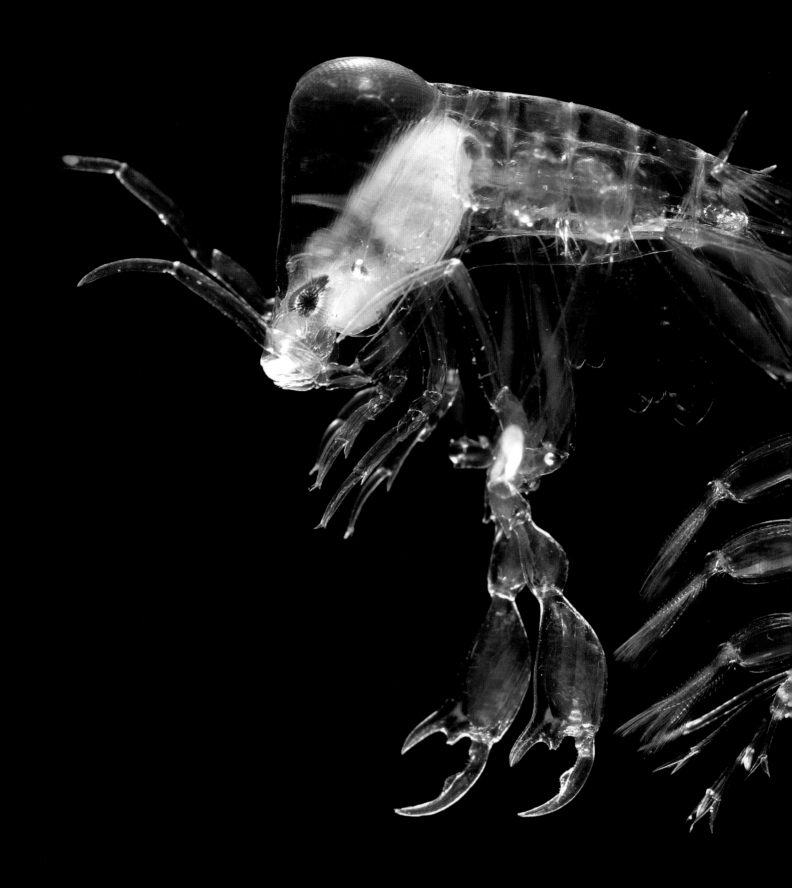

Pram bug

Phronima sp.

Size: 2 centimetres

The pram bug has been cited as the inspiration for at least one Hollywood alien. These charismatic amphipods normally reside within the hollowed-out body of a barrel salp, a type of deep-sea jelly. To make its home, the pram bug consumes the hapless salp's interior, before moving in and laying its eggs. Thus protected, the pram bug's family is safer than most animals in the exposed mid-water realm.

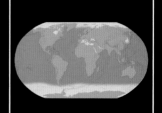

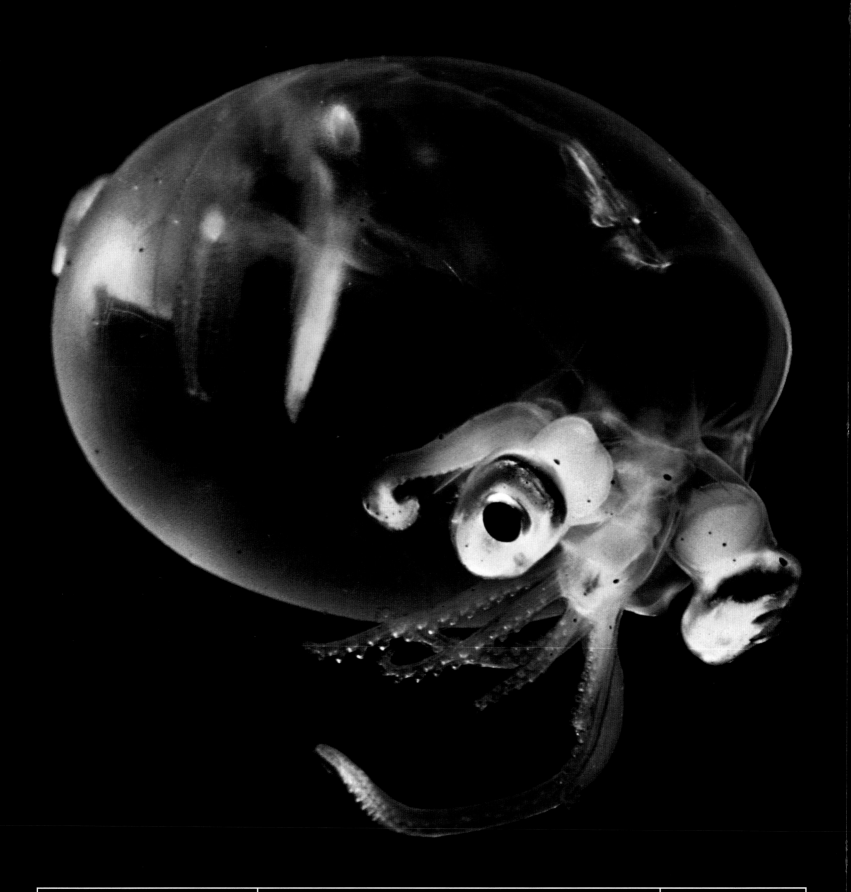

Glass squid

┌ 200 m

└ 1000 m

Teuthowenia pellucida
Size: 5 centimetres

The aliens are among us! The googly eyed glass squid has a face drawn straight from science fiction, yet it is a real and important deep-sea species of the temperate southern hemisphere. Juveniles have eyes set on stalks, but as the squid grows to its adult size of about 20 centimetres the stalks shorten and disappear.

Glass squid balling

200 m

1000 m

Teuthowenia pellucida
Size: 5 centimetres

Many deep-sea animals have distinctive ways of avoiding the ever-present threat of predators. When alarmed, this normally slender googly eyed squid inflates its body cavity with water, swelling into a transparent sphere. If the threat remains, the squid draws its head, arms and tentacles into its body and squirts ink into it, becoming a black ball hanging in the darkness.

Giant squid

300 m

1000 m

Architeuthis dux
Size: 12 metres

A diver encounters a pair of fully grown giant squid in this fanciful artwork, which nonetheless conveys the size of these immense molluscs. Living at depths between 300 and 1,000 metres, they feed upon smaller squid and fishes, growing to 12 metres in length. Still to be properly photographed in its natural habitat, the giant squid remains a powerful symbol of how little we know about deep-sea life.

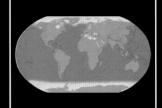

Colossal squid

┌ 200 m
│
│
│
└ 4000 m

Mesonychoteuthis
hamiltoni
Size: 10 metres

In 2007, a previously obscure species of squid stole the record of 'world's largest invertebrate' from the giant squid. In the frigid waters surrounding Antarctica, a colossal squid weighing about half a tonne was captured, breaking the previous weight record by about 200 kilograms. Armed with hook-like talons and short muscular arms, it preys on human-sized Patagonian toothfish.

Pelagic amphipod

200 m

1000 m

Cyphocaris sp.
Size: 1.5 centimetres

A mass of limbs and appendages, this amphipod is a frenetic sight as it swims. These mid-water crustaceans snatch fish eggs and other planktonic prey from the water column and can produce bright flashes of bioluminescence from their head and tail regions. As with other amphipods, the eggs develop inside a special pouch called a marsupium, located on the female's underside.

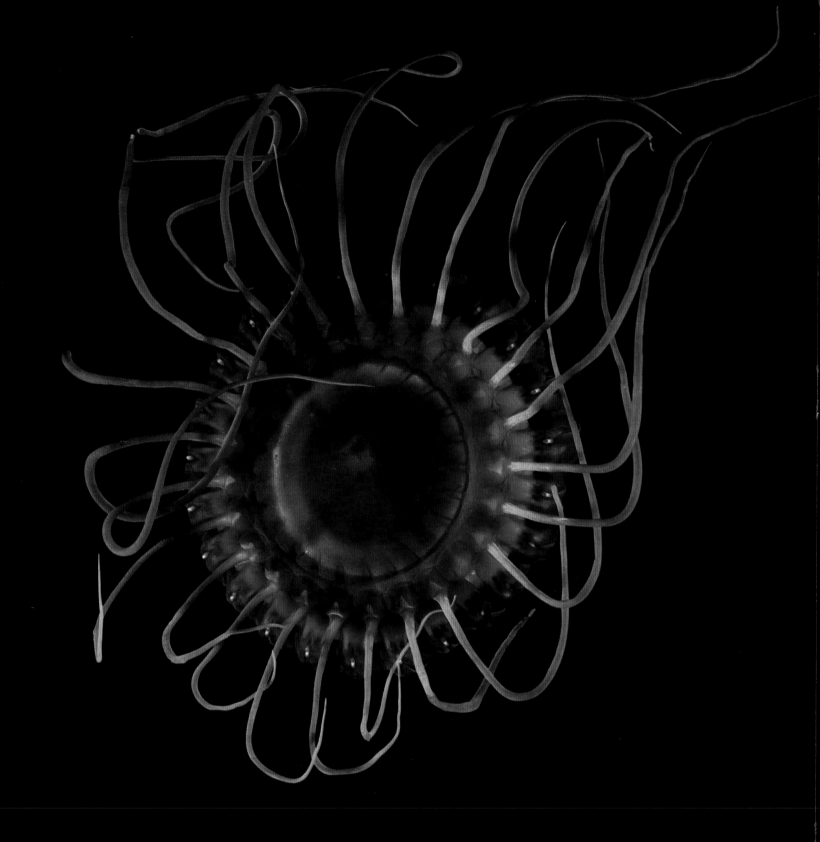

Crown jellyfish

200 m
4000 m

Atolla sp
Size: 3 centimetres

This bioluminescent jellyfish is just one of many species of deep-sea jellies. Its striking red colouration is a common feature among the many inhabitants of the ocean's twilight zone. The explanation? Red wavelengths of light cannot penetrate far in seawater; at depth, animals coloured red actually appear to be black or dark brown – effectively a form of camouflage in the dim blue light.

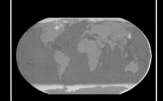

Deep-sea siphonophore

200 m

1000 m

Marrus orthocanna
Size: 15 centimetres

This delicate siphonophore jelly is actually a colony composed of many individuals, each one modified for a specific task, such as swimming or feeding. From a practical point of view, however, the individuals in the colony are cooperating so closely that the siphonophore behaves as a single organism.

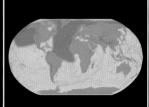

Black seadevil

200 m

4000 m

Melanocetus johnsonii
Size: 8 centimetres

The black seadevil, *Melanocetus johnsonii*, has a gaping maw lined with outsized sabre-like teeth. Be thankful this nightmarish species grows to a maximum size of 15 centimetres. Using its glowing lure – actually a modified dorsal fin spine – the black seadevil can ambush prey larger than itself: one seven-centimetre black seadevil was found with a 24-centimetre viperfish in its stomach.

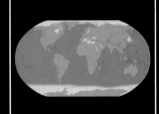

Hydrothermal vent

1000 m

4500 m

In this illustration, a hydrothermal vent spews super-heated black 'smoke' through several chimneys made of precipitated minerals, three kilometres down. Clustered around the vent is a profusion of life, including giant tubeworms, giant clams and vent mussels. These species rely upon symbiotic bacteria to convert the chemical energy in the vent fluids into usable energy.

Vent crab

```
┌ 1000 m
│
└ 4000 m
```

Bythograea thermydron
Size: 7 centimetres

Occurring in their hundreds around actively smoking chimneys, this crab is one of the vent's top predators. Opportunistic feeders, they browse on clumps of bacteria and are not above nipping the tips off the feeding plumes of giant tubeworms (p196). When the crabs' planktonic larvae settle on the sea floor, their eyes are remodelled to detect the infrared light emitted by the black smokers.

Squat lobster

1000 m

Munidopsis sp.
Size: 5 centimetres

From muddy abyssal plains to the rusting interior of the *Titanic* wreck, to the simmering heat of black smokers, squat lobsters are seen virtually everywhere in the deep. Their albino colouring and long, forward-pointing pincers make these opportunistic predators instantly recognizable. Despite their name they are not true lobsters, b   a   e closely related to hermit crabs.

Giant tubeworm

1000 m

Riftia pachyptila
Size: 2 metres

An emblem of all unknown life on Earth, the giant tubeworm was discovered in the late 1970s, along with the hydrothermal vents they inhabit. Initial confusion about how these three-metre long worms grew to such great sizes without a mouth, gut or anus was solved when researchers discovered the worms relied

Jericho worm

1000 m

4000 m

Tevnia jerichonana

Size: 30 centimetres

The plume of a Jericho worm protrudes from its papery tube. Like the giant tubeworm *Riftia*, this hydrothermal vent dweller also harbours symbiotic bacteria. Composed of sheets of fine tentacles, the plume acts as a gill that absorbs the chemical ingredients – sulphide, carbon dioxide and oxygen – employed by the worm's colony of bacteria to grow and feed their host.

Vent eelpout

1000 m

4000 m

Thermarces cerberus
Size: 30 centimetres

The eelpout, *Thermarces cerberus*, is one of several fishes found only on hydrothermal vents. Interesting to scientists, but infuriatingly difficult to catch for submersible pilots, these saggy skinned, 30-centimetre long fishes are usually seen nestling among masses of giant tubeworms. Taking advantage of their rich habitat, the eelpout hunts a wide range of prey, including the tubeworms themselves.

Deep-sea anemone

1000 m

4000 m

Not known
Size: 5 centimetres

An unidentified anemone encountered by the famed submersible *Alvin* during a dive to Chowder Hill, an area of venting two kilometres deep on the Juan de Fuca Ridge, off British Columbia. As vibrant as any showy anemone living atop a coral reef, the animal's presence on a lump of volcanic basalt in a realm of eternal darkness made it an especially striking sight.

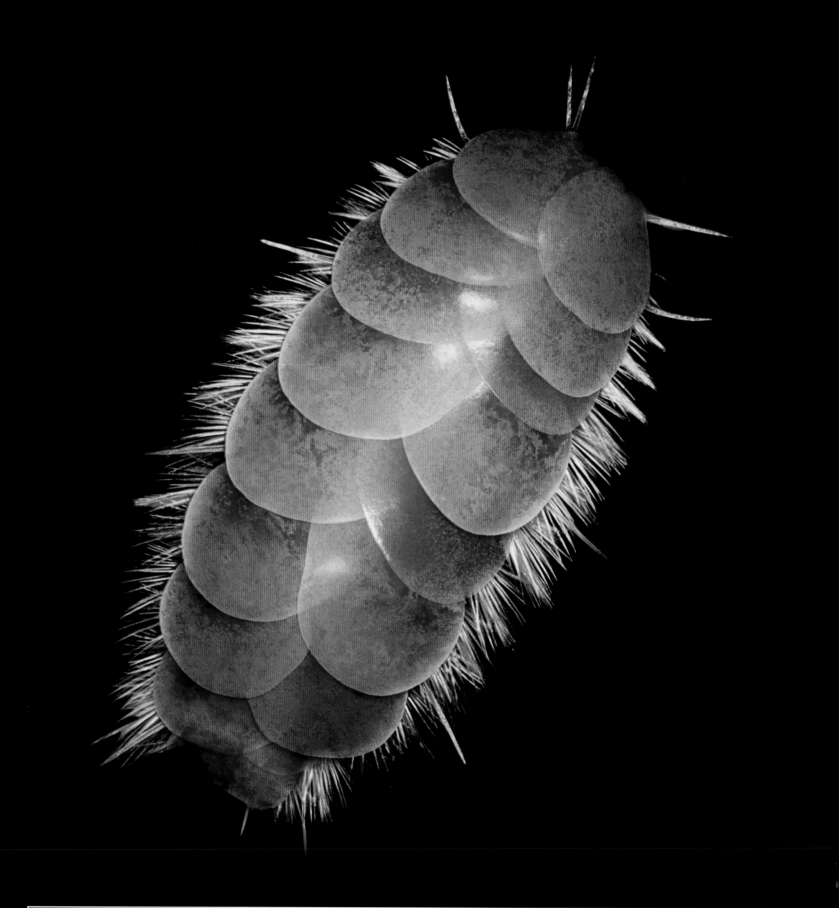

Vent scaleworm

1000 m
4000 m

Family Polynoidae
Size: 2.5 centimetres

Easily recognized by their distinctive scales, vent scaleworms are a successful family whose myriad species have colonized coastal shallows as well as deep ocean trenches. They are particularly diverse on hydrothermal vents, where some species crawl in their hundreds over black-smoker chimneys, hunting shrimps or grazing on bacteria, while others live symbiotically inside vent mussels.

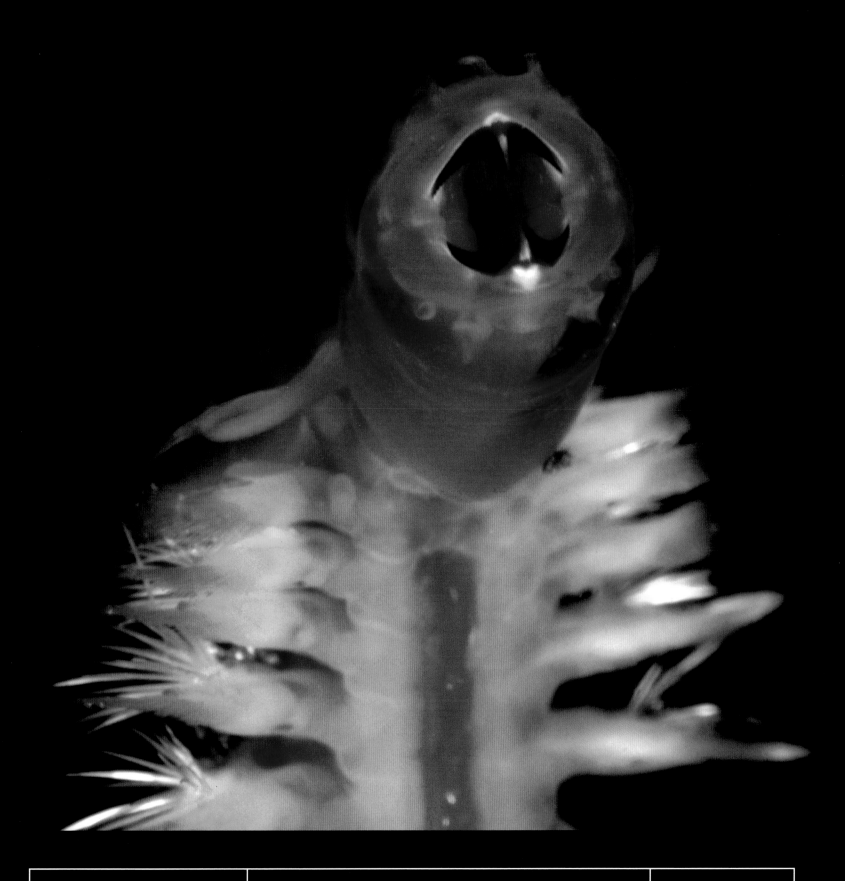

Vent scaleworm jaws

1000 m

4000 m

Family Polynoidae
Size: 2.5 centimetres

The sharp, parrot-like jaws of the same vent scaleworm pictured left reflect a predatory lifestyle, and these roving predators are surprisingly fast and agile. They can even swim by undulating their bodies from side to side, rowing through the water column, their stiff bunches of bristles acting as oars.

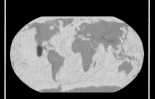

Vent mussel shell

1000 m

Bathymodiolus sp.
Size: 30 centimetres

4000 m

A vent mussel shell is home to a variety of small creatures: brittlestars, limpets and a worm. Black smoker communities are busy places, the biological equivalent of New York City, where a concentration of resources attracts great numbers and diversity. At least 500 vent species have been recorded – and to date only a tiny percentage of these undersea hot springs have been explored.

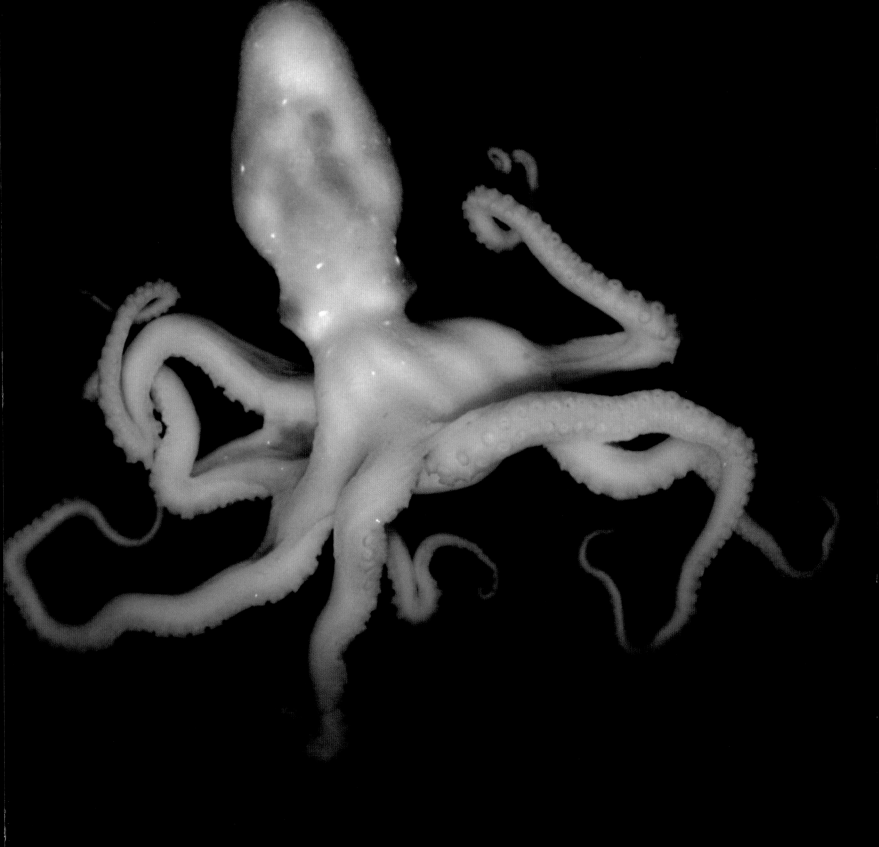

Vent octopus

```
┌ 1000 m
│
│
└ 4000 m
```

Vulcanoctopus hydrothermalis
Size: 12 centimetres

Only found on eastern Pacific black smokers, these diminutive octopuses specialize in catching swarms of small vent amphipods. The pale flecks on its body are copepod crustaceans embedded under the octopus's skin. For some reason males are particularly vulnerable to these rather unpleasant parasites.

Pompeii worm

1000 m

4000 m

Alvinella pompejana
Size: 10 centimetres

Some like it hot: Pompeii worms can tolerate the highest temperatures of any known animal, up to 80°C, enabling them to form dense colonies close to the super-heated tips of black smoker chimneys. The worms secrete papery tubes that form a chaotic honeycomb, and subsist on free-living vent bacteria.

Pompeii worm

1000 m
—4000 m

Alvinella pompejana
Size: 10 centimetres

Seen up close, the shaggy fur of the Pompeii worm is revealed to be hairs coated by dense colonies of fluffy white bacteria. Locked into a symbiotic relationship with the host worm, the mucus-secreting bacteria may serve as an insulating coat, providing temporary relief from the high temperatures and toxic chemicals found on the black smokers where the Pompeii worm lives.

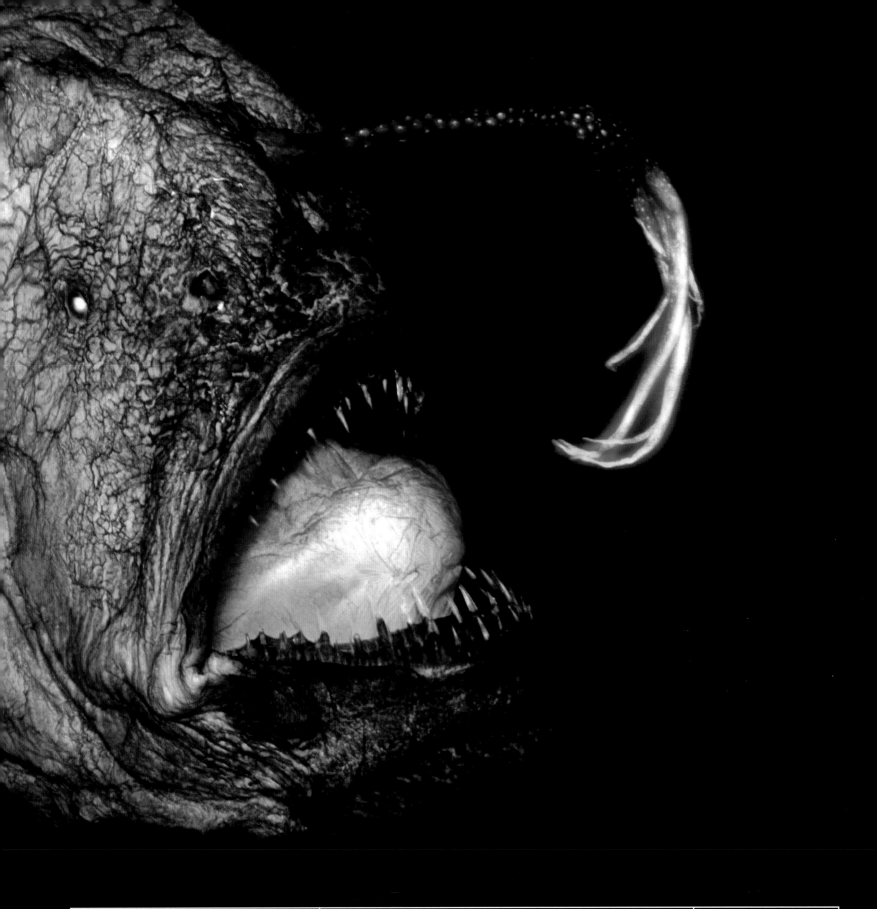

Atlantic footballfish

┌─ 1000 m
│
│   *Himantolophus groenlandicus*
│   Size: 25 centimètres
│
└─ 4000 m

Sporting a lure shaped eerily like a skeletal claw, the footballfish is one of the deep's many lurking predators. Females grow to the size of, strangely enough, a football, while males are only a fraction of this size. Although there are many species of anglers, individual fishes are very thinly distributed in the water column and rarely encounter each other.

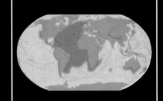

Dumbo octopus

1000 m

>4000 m

Grimpoteuthis sp.
Size: 15 centimetres

An unofficial mascot of deep-diving submariners, the exquisite Dumbo octopus lives on and above the abyssal sea floor. It is so-named for its ear-like fins, which flap like wings – prompting an obvious comparison with Disney's much-loved elephant. Strangely deliberate in their movements, Dumbos often perform delicate contortions before jetting slowly off into the darkness.

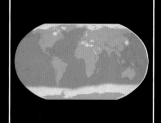

Hairy anglerfish

Caulophryne sp
Size: 20 centimetres

Hanging silently in the abyss, the hairy anglerfish is a vision of lurking malevolence. Its hairy projections act as tripwires, enabling it to sense the vibrations of possible prey. Like other deep-sea anglers it bears a glowing lure to attract prey. The females are proportionally huge, and the males are small and parasitic, attaching to the females and ultimately fusing with her bloodstream.

Loosejaw

1000 m

3000 m

Aristostomias sp.
Size: 17 centimetres

Slung beneath the eye of the loosejaw fish is a prominent red-hued light organ.
It functions as a searchlight, exposing prey hidden in the darkness. Most deep-sea
animals cannot see red, but in an elegant evolutionary arrangement, the loosejaw's
eyes can detect the very wavelength emitted by the organ beneath them. In effect, it
is wearing night-vision goggles; it can see others without betraying its own position.

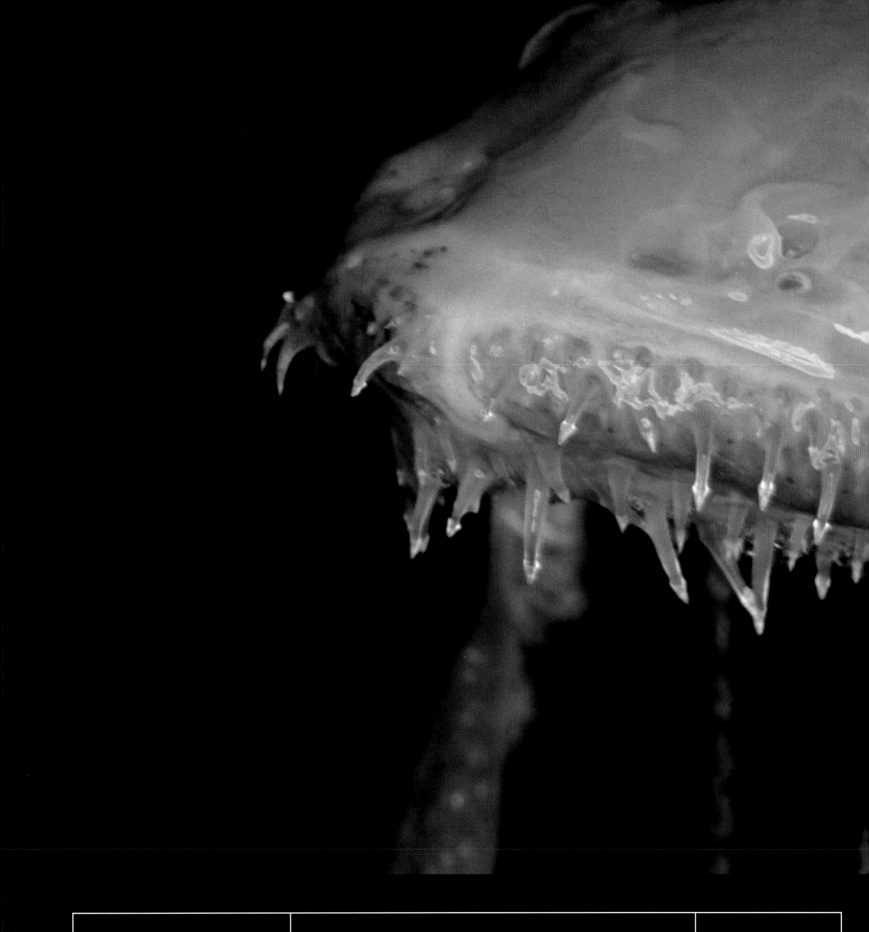

Highfin lizardfish

1000 m

>4000 m

Bathysaurus mollis
Size: 30 centimetres

Living a sedentary life on the deep-sea floor *Bathysaurus*, or 'deep lizard', is the consummate ambush predator. Quick jaws and harpoon-tipped teeth seize any prey that strays too close, while additional hinging teeth on the roof of the mouth ratchet struggling victims down the lizardfish's throat. Not built for speed, these sluggish creatures can be collected by the mechanical claws of deep-diving ROVs.

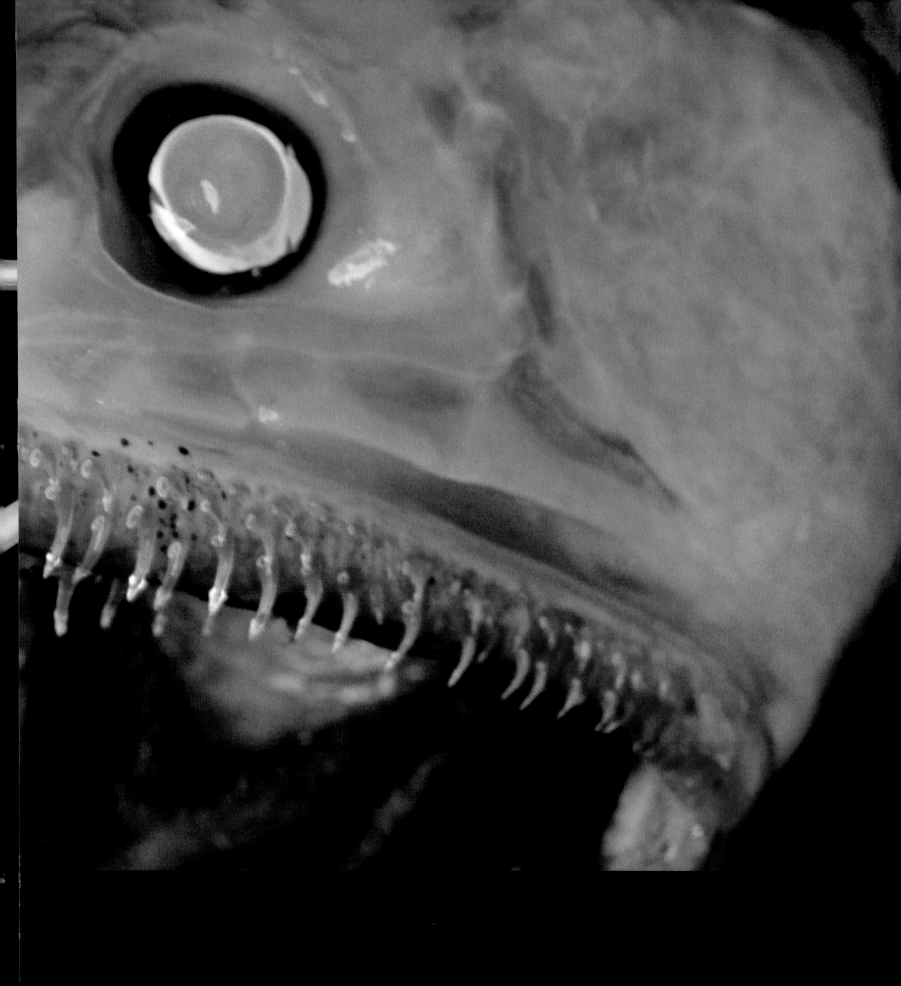

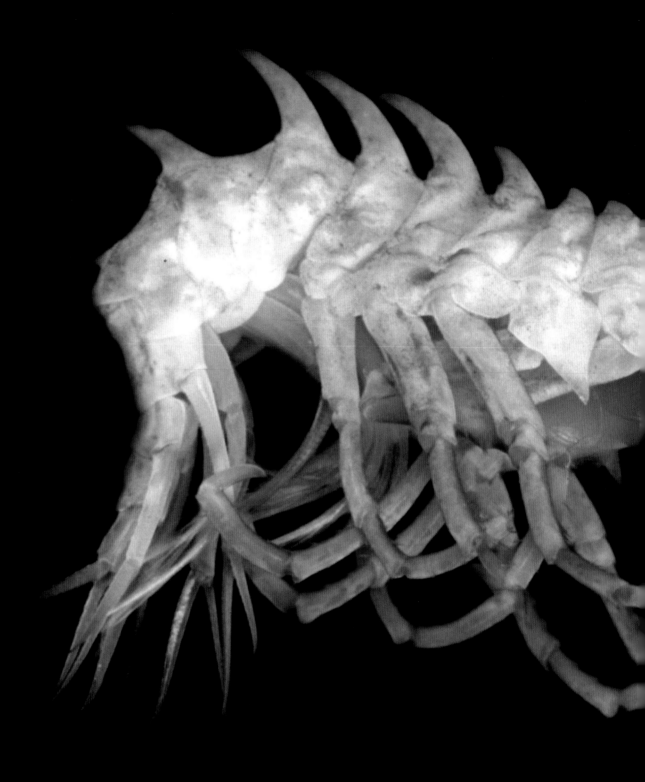

Eusirid amphipod

1000 m

>4000m

Family Eusiridae

Size: 2 centimetres

On the deepest abyssal plains and in the deep ocean trenches, amphipods are usually the dominant mobile scavengers of the sea floor. Close relatives of the diminutive sandhoppers found in thousands beneath seaweed on sandy beaches, some deepwater forms grow nearly 20 centimetres long. The ornately sculpted amphipod here has curved legs enabling it to grasp the stalks of glass sponges.

Bathyscaphe *Trieste*

┌─ 0 m
│
└─ −10,911 m

Size: 15 metres

Our journey into the deep ends here, nearly 11 kilometres down at Challenger Deep in the Mariana Trench. But does life exist at such extreme depths? This fundamental question was answered in 1960, when Don Walsh and Jacques Piccard arrived in the bathyscaphe *Trieste*. Moments before touchdown obscured the sea floor with a cloud of fine mud, Piccard sighted a flatfish scooting across the pale sediments.

Glossary

ABYSS The region of the ocean deeper than 3,000 metres.

ADAPTATION The means by which a living organism or species changes form or behaviour to become better suited to its environment.

AMENSALISM A symbiotic relationship between two organisms in which one partner is not affected while the other is harmed.

BATHYSCAPHE a deep-diving submarine able to dive to great depths using a gasoline-filled float for buoyancy. The most famous bathyscaph was the *Trieste*, which set the world depth record of 10,915 metres in the Marianas Trench.

BLACK SMOKERS Hydrothermal vents found on ocean ridges that emit hot, mineral-laden fluids, often from chimney-like structures. Home to a unique chemosynthetic ecosystem.

BENTHIC The habit of living on or within the sea floor.

BIOLUMINESCENCE Cold light produced by many marine animals by a chemical reaction. Compare with fluorescence.

BIOMASS Refers to the total mass of living things within a particular area.

CAMOUFLAGE An animal's ability to blend in with the environment to avoid detection by other animals.

CARNIVORE Animal that feeds on the flesh of other animals, either hunted or scavenged.

CEPHALOPOD The class of sophisticated and often intelligent marine molluscs that includes octopuses and squid.

CHEMOSYNTHESIS The method used by some marine bacteria to harvest energy contained within inorganic chemicals such as hydrogen sulphide. Chemosynthesis is the basis of the life found at hydrothermal vents.

COMMENSALISM The relationship between two organisms in which one gains a benefit while the other is neither helped nor harmed.

CONTINENTAL SHELF The shallow, near flat rim that surrounds most of the continents. Normally tens or hundreds of kilometres wide, its outer edge drops off at around 200 metres deep, where the continental slope begins.

CONTINENTAL SLOPE The steep slope that separates the continental shelf from the deep-sea floor.

COPEPOD 'Insects of the sea', these small crustaceans make up a major fraction of the zooplankton throughout the ocean.

DEEP SEA Many definitions exist, but most scientists agree that the deep sea is that part of the ocean deeper than 200 metres.

DIATOM Important microscopic phytoplankton with shells made of glass.

DINOFLAGELLATE Actively swimming phytoplankton. Some dinoflagellates are notorious for forming toxic blooms.

DIURNAL Day-active rather than night-active (nocturnal).

ECOSYSTEM The interconnected community of organisms and physical environment in which they live.

ENDEMIC When a species is found only in a certain area and nowhere else.

EXOSKELETON External rigid covering that supports the body of an invertebrate animal.

DETRITUS Organic particles formed through decomposition of organisms or their faecal matter.

DETRIVORE An animal that feeds on decomposing organic matter, or detritus.

DIVERSITY The variety of organisms in an ecosystem.

DOWNWELLING When surface seawater evaporates, it leaves its salt contents behind. As a result the salt-enriched water becomes denser than the surrounding water and begins to sink – causing downwelling (opposite to upwelling).

FILTER FEEDERS Suspension feeders that collect small or microscopic particles from the water column.

FLUORESCENCE The phenomenon by which some substances (including the surface of certain marine animals) emit visible light when exposed to ultraviolet light.

FOOD CHAIN The sequence by which organisms in an ecosystem eat and are eaten. For example: phytoplankton, copepod, fish, dolphin.

GONADS An animal's reproductive organs that produce eggs or sperm.

GYRE Giant ocean-wide currents that move in a circular direction. There are five gyres in the world's oceans.

HABITAT The place an organism lives.

HERMAPHRODITE An organism that has sexual organs of both genders – a common arrangement among many invertebrates and fishes.

HERBIVORE An animal that grazes on plants or algae.

HYDROTHERMAL VENT An undersea hot spring, in which heated water, often rich in dissolved minerals, flows out of fissures in the sea floor.

INTERTIDAL The zone on the seashore that lies between the high-tide and low-tide mark.

INVERTEBRATES Animal without a spinal column or backbone. More than 95 percent of all animals are invertebrates.

JELLIES Collective name for many different kinds of zooplankton that have gelatinous bodies. Examples include salps, jellyfish, and comb jellies.

KEYSTONE SPECIES A species that has large influence on the community in which it lives.

MARINE Describes anything associated with the ocean.

MESOPELAGIC ZONE The 'twilight' layer of the ocean, where there is faint light during the day, but not quite enough for plants to grow.

MUTUALISM A symbiotic relationship between individuals of two different species, in which both partners benefit.

NOCTURNAL Animals that are active during the night.

OMNIVORE An animal that is able to feed on a diverse diet of both plant and animal food.

OVIPAROUS When female organisms lay eggs rather than giving birth to live young. This is the dominant form of reproduction in the sea.

PARASITISM A symbiotic relationship between individuals of two different species, in which one partner benefits and the other is harmed.

PELAGIC Pelagic organisms are those that live in the water column, rather than on the sea floor.

PHOTIC ZONE The surface layer of the ocean, where there is enough sunlight for seaweeds and phytoplankton to grow.

PHOTOSYNTHESIS The chemical reaction plants use to convert solar energy into food.

PHYTOPLANKTON Microscopic organisms that drift in the ocean and engage in photosynthesis. They are usually invisible to the human eye, but can occur in dense blooms that give seawater a green, brown, white or red tint.

PLANKTON Organisms that live suspended in the water column and drift with the currents rather than travel by their own locomotion.

POPULATION A community of organisms of the same species that live in a particular place.

SEDIMENT Particles of rock or shelly material that are transported by the fluid motion of rivers, oceans, glaciers and even wind and are eventually deposited on the sea floor. Sediments are classified by size, and include mud, sand and gravel.

SUSPENSION FEEDER Animals that collect and feed upon plankton or organic particles from the water column.

SHORELINE Where the land meets the sea.

SPLASH ZONE The area on the shore above the high tide mark but still affected by salt-water splashes.

SYMBIOSIS When organisms of different species live in close proximity to each other.

TEMPERATE The climate zone between the polar region and the subtropical zone. Mild but with clear seasons.

TIDE The periodic rising and falling of the level of the ocean due to the gravitational pull of the moon and the sun.

TERRESTRIAL An inhabitant of the land.

TROPICAL Hot and humid zone around the equator.

UPWELLING When deep waters are pushed up towards the surface. Often, upwelled waters are rich in life.

VIVIPAROUS When female organisms give birth to live, well-developed young.

ZOOPLANKTON Animal plankton.

Index

To our daughters: Amy and Marlene

ACKNOWLEDGEMENTS

The authors thank DeepOcean Quest for support during the writing of this book. We are also grateful for assistance from Alison McDiarmid, Brian Batson, David Batson, Kim Westerskov, Mike McDowell and all the contributing photographers.

PHOTO CREDITS

David Batson / DeepSeaPhotography.com: 21; 186-187; 188; 193; 218-219.
Peter Batson / DeepSeaPhotography.com: 19; 41; 53; 154; 173; 176; 177; 182; 183; 184; 189; 194; 195; 196; 197; 198; 199; 200; 201; 202; 203; 204; 205; 206; 207; 208; 209; 212-213; 214; 215; 216-217; 222-223. Nicolas Cheetham / data from Blue Marble Next Generation courtesy of Reto Stöckli / NASA Earth Observatory: 7; Phillip Colla / Phillip Colla Photography: 30-31; 38-39; 61; 90; 110-111; 116-117; 148; 149; 158-159; 160-161; 162-163; 164-165; 168; 174-175. Jürgen Freund / Freund Factory: 11; 15; 24; 25; 26; 27; 28-29; 43; 46-47; 59; 60; 63; 65; 66; 68-69; 70; 71; 72; 73; 74; 75; 76; 77; 78; 80; 81; 82-83; 84; 85; 86; 88-89; 91; 93; 95; 95; 97; 98; 99; 100; 101; 102-103; 104; 106; 107; 108-109; 112; 113; 114; 115; 118-119; 150; 151; 156; 157; 185. Steven Haddock / DeepSeaPhotography.Com: 2-3; 178-179. Paul Nicklen / Paul Nicklen Photography: 43; 94; 130-131; 132; 133; 140; 141; 142; 143; 170-171. Kevin Raskoff / DeepSeaPhotography.Com: 138; 139; 191. David Shale / DeepSeaPhotography.Com: 155; 180; 181; 190; 192; 210; 211. Reto Stöckli / NASA Earth Observatory: 8-9; David Wachenfeld / Triggerfish Images: 67; 79; 87. Kim Westerskov / Natural Images: 12; 16-17; 20; 22; 23; 32; 33; 34-35; 36; 37; 42; 45; 48; 49; 50-51; 52; 54-55; 56-57; 58; 64; 92; 121; 122; 123; 124; 125; 126-127; 134; 135; 144-145; 147; 152; 153; 169. Norbert Wu / Norbert Wu Productions: 105; 136, 128; 129 137; 166-167.

Quercus
21 Bloomsbury Square
London
WC1A 2NS

First published in 2008

Copyright © Quercus Publishing Ltd 2008

A catalogue record for this book is available from the British Library.

ISBN (UK): 978-1-84724-050-7
ISBN (US): 978-1-84724-144-3

Printed and bound in China